DISCRIMINATION AGAINST GIRL CHILD

DISCRIMINATION AGAINST GIRL CHILD

The Trajectory of Missing Girls

MOLY KURUVILLA

GYAN

Discrimination Against Girl Child : The Trajectory of Missing Girls

ISBN: 978-81-212-1132-1

Published in 2011 in India by
Gyan Publishing House
23, Main Ansari Road, Darya Ganj
New Delhi-110002
Phones : 23282060, 23261060
Fax : 011-23285914
E-mail: books@gyanbooks.com
Website: www.gyanbooks.com

Laser Type Setting by: Rudra Computer Graphics, Delhi
Printed at : Chawla Offset Printers, Delhi

To millions of my sisters who struggle hard
to hold their heads high and
to live a life with dignity

Contents

Contents

Foreword

When Dr. Moly Kuruvilla, Reader i/c Director, Centre for Women's Studies, University of Calicut, approached me with a request that I write a 'Foreword' for her book *"Discrimination Against Girl Child: The Trajectory of Missing Girls"*, at first I tried to dissuade her. I told her that she should ask some of the other eminent experts in the country known for their contributions in the cause of fighting injustice against women.

However, Dr. Moly Kuruvilla was successful in finally persuading me to agree to her request. She argued that being a former 'Justice' and presently the Chairperson of the Kerala State Women's Commission, I was her right choice. The judgments delivered while in active service and having the experience and exposure of several years as a responsible and responsive person in dealing with the injustices against women, is the sole reason for seeking my involvement, she stated.

Kerala is the only state in the country, which shows a fairly good sex ratio in favor of women. The god's own country with its high human development indices such as low maternal mortality, low infant mortality, low fertility rates and high literacy rate occupies the status of a model state as far as women development is concerned. But the book highlights the unfavourable child sex ratio and exposes the phenomenon of feminisation of the old and masculinisation of the young in the state.

The book deals with the subject of son preference and female foeticide supported by in depth research and quoting various well-known authorities. I would like to congratulate Dr. Moly Kuruvilla for the efforts she has taken to undertake a study on a quite relevant theme of declining child sex ratio in the state and writng a book with sufficient content on the what, why and how of empowering girls and women. Her ideas on enhancing the dignity of girl child will be useful to clarify the misconceptions of thousands of men and women regarding why our accelerated women empowerment programmes fail to attain the desired targets.

The various atrocities perpetrated, in spite of legislations and policies drawn up by the Union Government and State Governments, are really a challenge to the implementation of law and order and a threat to the basic decency and fundamental rights of all human beings as guaranteed by our Constitution. The lesson for us to follow is that by enacting policies and passing stringent laws, we are not going to stop the crimes against women and enhance their dignity. What we need is a wide spread awareness campaign to drive home the facts regarding gender discrimination truthfully so as to change the existing patriarchal mindsets and expose the evil doers. All sections of society must join hands to put an end to this ever-growing menace.

Justice (Retd.) D. Sreedevi
Chairperson
The Kerala State Women's Commission

Preface

We take pride in living in the twenty-first century and never cease talking about the advancements made. The information technology explosion and innovations in various disciplines have made it possible for us to cross international borders in no time at all and we could be sitting at each other's doorsteps in a matter of hours. Today, our world has become one global village. But, on the other hand this much touted technological advance is being misused to eliminate female foetus in the womb itself, murder by compulsion and use of force at the hands of ruthless criminals bred by a patriarchal society, urban, rural, rich and poor alike.

It all began when I came across a heartbreaking and captivating rendering of personal agony by a senior speaker at one of the seminars where I too was one of the speakers. The experiences shared by her, with her permission, in all honesty I have narrated in the first few pages of the book, for the benefit of fellow women and their families who may be in similar or worse situations. In my opinion it will be a useful lesson if well learned and the time one invest in imbibing the contents is not at all going to be a waste. Further, my intention in sharing this painful tragedy with my readers is to make them realize and create an awareness of what is taking place in many a house behind closed doors. Once the realization strikes home, I am sure there will be caring, willing, decent human beings who will come forward to lend a hand and support any movement to alleviate the sufferings. Anyone with an iota of conscience will not look the other way.

The experiences of this great woman motivated me to take up an investigation on the extent of son preference and to trace the presence of female foeticide which might form a reason for the unfavourable child sex ratio in the glorified society.

The state of Kerala, God's Own Country, projects a glorified picture of a model state with regard to women's development. The high human development indices related to women are comparable to those of the developed west. Kerala's reproductive health index, low infant mortality, low maternal mortality, low fertility rates and above all, the cent percent literacy rate and high educational standards of producing the highest number of doctors, engineers and IT professionals, all make the society an elite one among the rest of the states.

Despite all these achievements, the statistics on rape, domestic violence, dowry deaths, pornography scandals and sexual abuse make Kerala a terrible place for women to live in. This unfortunate situation and by extension the declining trend in the child sex ratio of Kerala fails to receive the deserving importance and attention of the activists and policy makers. I will be very happy if this publication throws further light on the truth behind the curtain of women development indices of Kerala.

The methodology adopted for the study along with the analysis and results are given in detail so that the book will be useful as a reference text for students in Women's Studies, Sociology, Anthropology and Social Work and NGO's and social workers to repeat the same in their own regions and make possible comparisons and design effective measures to curb the evil.

In the last few pages on *'Enhancing the Status and Dignity of Girl Child',* I have listed almost all queries that spring up in the seminars and workshops aimed at the same. It is hoped that the discussion will be extremely useful to all concerned, especially those who are working at the grassroot level. Hundreds of women like Preraks of the National Literacy Mission, Anganwadi workers and Ashas of the National Rural Health Mission have made repeated requests for making such a comprehensive attempt on the various aspects of women's emancipation as dealt with in the last part.

The life story of Vanitha reveals how a postgraduate degree with a high first class and a huge package of dowry failed to contribute anything in enhancing the dignity of a Keralite girl, especially in her husband's home. In the last chapter, Vanitha's example itself is depicted to highlight how economic independence along with a strong determination would enable a woman to rise up from the status of a doormat to that of a woman leader living a life with dignity, so as to provide a motivation to every woman in distress.

If the contents of the book find some place in helping those, both men and women, who are ready to link their destinies with those of the millions of women who need to be awakened and helped to lead empowered lives to make a difference, the purpose is attained. The unleashing of a mammoth awareness campaign with the involvement of all concerned bodies and with the full support of the governments at Centre and States can surely help. Strict monitoring, professional evaluation and follow- up action are a must. Let us hope one day soon our joint efforts will become fruitful and alleviate the sufferings of thousands and millions of women behind the closed doors.

Dr. Moly Kuruvilla
Reader i/c Director
Centre for Women's Studies
University of Calicut
Kerala-673635

Acknowledgements

First and foremost I would like to express my sincere thanks to my new friend who dared to share her personal experiences with me and granted permission to share them with all the readers so as to sensitise them with what is going on in the life of many a woman.

I am extremely grateful to Justice (Retd.) D. Sreedevi, the Chairperson of Kerala State Women's Commission who has written the 'Foreword' for this Book and has always been a role model and constant support in my efforts to alleviate the sufferings of fellow women.

My sincere thanks are due to Prof. Anwar Jahan Zuberi, the former Vice Chancellor of University of Calicut who has inspired me to write more and more on women's issues and has offered valuable tips in the publication of this work.

The author places it on record her gratitude to Prof. N. Kala, Mother Teresa Women's University, Kodaikanal for the guidance and encouragement rendered by her during the execution of the self initiated project on Missing Girls in Kerala. A part of the project was submitted as Dissertation and was highly recommended for the award ofthe Degree of M.Phil in Women's Studies of the University to the author.

The author expresses her sincere thanks to:

Dr. P.A. Lalitha, Malabar Hospital, Kozhikode
Dr. Kadija Mumthas, Medical College Hospital, Kozhikode
Dr. Asha Muhammed, Feroke College, Kozhikode
Smt. Maleeha Raghaviah, Journalist, Kozhikode and
Sri. K.R. Menon, Adviser - PR & Editorial, Kozhikode for their contributions in the form of anecdotal inputs, proof reading, editing etc. without which the Book wouldn't have become a reality.

Moly Kuruvilla

1

An Untold Story

The aroma of freshly brewed black coffee filled the air and my new friend sipping her coffee looked deep into my eyes. I returned the gaze assuring trustworthiness and confidentiality. The ambience was soothing yet foreboding. I had met her on the very first day of a three day seminar on Women Empowerment: Challenges and Strategies. This was the beginning of yet another lesson for me as a counselor and germination of an idea for documentation, based on my friend's brutal and traumatic life and times. The nature stood still with abated breath for her story to unfold..... What follows here is not fiction but a real life story.

Her talk at the seminar had kept the audience riveted to their seats and at the tea-break she was surrounded by eager participants, who were vying with each other for her attention and closer interaction. Our informal chat over dinner helped pave the way for us to meet, even as late as 11 PM, the next day evening. Her revelations were really shocking and an eye-opener. Then and there I took her permission to narrate her harrowing experience for the benefit of all who find themselves in similar situations.

Let's go back in time. Twenty years ago this simple and innocent village beauty was given in marriage by her parents to a young, handsome and rich Malayalee businessman in Bhopal. She was very happy little knowing what shock awaited her in her wedded life. The first twelve months flew away and the couple enjoyed every moment. For the convenience of this narration let me name my friend 'Vanitha' meaning 'woman'.

Fate struck the first blow when Vanitha was in her second month of pregnancy. One evening her husband arrived with two tickets for them to go to Bombay (now Mumbai) to do an Amniocentesis laboratory test to determine the sex of the child in her womb. Vanitha was thrilled since she was also eager to know whether she was going to have a boy or girl. She was already planning her pregnancy, what to do and what not to do including purchase of comfortable clothes for the baby and a welcome celebration for the first born. Her happiness was short lived. Vanitha's husband told her that if she was carrying a female foetus, then she will have to undergo a Medical Termination of Pregnancy (MTP). Taken aback, she asked her husband what happens if she was unable to conceive again as a result of the MTP. Such incidents were known to happen.....she narrated an incident she had read. He had no convincing answer and in anger he tore and threw away the Mumbai tickets without waiting for her to finish with the details. This was the Beginning of the end.

In the eighth month of pregnancy, as custom demanded, Vanitha was sent to her native place for delivery. Mother-in-law seeing her small abdomen predicted a male child and the never ending discussion on the sex of the child every evening became a nightmare for my friend. At last the D-day arrived and she was hospitalized. The hue and cry that followed the child birth made the staff and other patients wonder if the mother had passed away at the time of delivery. Vanitha, in her sedated state, could vaguely hear her elder sister saying that a boy or a girl made no difference now. And the rejoinder from Vanitha's sister-in-law, contesting the issue, firmly asserting that a boy is a boy and a girl is simply a girl. Vanitha's husband on arrival took one look at the child in the cradle and went out with tears flowing down his cheeks. The next six days he spent with the mother and child, reluctantly leaving them on the seventh day for his trip back to Bhopal.

After observing the customary practices, on the 89th day, the husband took Vanitha and the baby girl to Bhopal. There was considerable change in her husband. At first she attributed her husband's behaviour to the addition in the family and increased responsibilities. But she was shocked when visitors told her that he had sold two of their factories to his partners and friends. The money from the sale was spent on liquor and such to forget his having fathered a female child. On being questioned why he didn't tell her about the sale, he replied that since he had bought the factories without her consent he saw no reason why he should tell her about the matter. This was indeed a blow to her.

The next three years Vanitha lived in hell and unspeakable horror. There was no let up in the physical, sexual, emotional and economic violence from her husband and his family. He made it a point to be home with friends to eat up every morsel of the cooked food leaving nothing for her or the baby. She had to live on very little, often drinking plain water; one of her innovations, to generate a little milk to breast feed the child!

Attempts to interfere with his shenanigans angered him to be crueler and beat up the wife left and right. He never let Vanitha forget her denial to undergo amniocenteses lab test. Time and again he reminded her that she was being punished for not obeying him.

My friend was slowly but steadily being forced to submission of his whims and fancies. Often one glass of rice was all she had to keep the hunger away for a whole week.......

But how come? I intervened. Being a typical product of patriarchy, he never let Vanitha to go out, either for shopping or visiting any friend. She was allowed to speak to friends only in his presence. When kitchen items were about to finish, her husband used to go out for picnicking with friends. With no money left at home Vanitha and the little girl were put to starve for days together. This made her recall what the poor ladies of the village used to say about giving their children the cooked rice and then their making do with the left over liquid (kanji).

From a healthy 58 kgs, her weight dropped down to an alarming 42 kgs. Even then she carried on taking care of her precious daughter. At no time did she inform her parents of her suffering, she recalls with pride. With no scope for contacting the world outside, practically no friends and relatives in the neighbourhood, she felt as if marooned in a remote island. Those were the days when she was in utter confusion ....whether to go back to parental home and enjoy all the richness, freedom and comforts or live with him enduring all insults and starvation. Finally she managed to convey the matter to one of those rare friends. She advised her to get a divorce from the husband. The very thought of having a fatherless child was shocking to her. She knew that leaving him for ever is begetting lifelong blame and endless torture. And what about her family prestige, the younger sister's marriage... she was not ready to sacrifice the happiness of the whole family because of her. But adjusting with him was no more possible.

It was then and there, on a fine morning when her husband left the home for his usual picnicking that she took that firm decision. ...Finishing off herself and the child. ..Vanitha still now recollects the momentum with which her thoughts and actions synchronised for an ending of everything. She cleaned the entire house....kept everything in order.....mopped the floors.....arranged the flower vases and kitchen wares in tact...bathed and dressed up the baby....had a bath of herself....put on her best chooridar with long duppatta... .everything was done in a hurry. ...she could hear the loud heart throbs but never waited for a second thought....said her final prayers....tied one end of the duppatta to the hooks on the ceiling. Everything was ready and she took the sleeping baby in her hands for the final kiss. At once the calling bell rang with a loud shocking bang. It won't be the husband, it won't be the part time maid. Slowly she came out of the bedroom without forgetting to close its door behind.

An unexpected guest waited outside, the young family friend from Kerala, who occasionally visited the family in the evenings. He was on an official tour to Switzerland, came back by noon and as per his version he had a dream about his little friend in one of those mild nap in the flight. Instead of going straight away to his apartment, he thought of dropping down for a few minutes and handing over the carefully chosen baby doll to the child. His visit ruined all her plans ...the entire incident started rewinding in her mind. She thought... 'God doesn't allow me to die....may be it is his wish that I endure all these pains ....but for what... I wondered for an answer'. After two hours when the child woke up from her nap Vanitha was a different person, a person with a new outlook on life, with a definite answer for her question. She made up her mind to fight the battle. She has to live at least for the sake of her daughter. Though her life is ruined, the little one has a long life to live, why not lend a helping hand in shaping a bright future for the neglected child.

Now Vanitha refers to her daughter as the 'Colour in her life'. "Yes, my daughter has added so much colour in my life, the only motivation for me to get on with the sufferings in the beginning, the reservoir of warmth and emotional support later on and my best friend today".

Again life went on as usual ...the interrogations.... insults.....poverty and slavery but now the feel was different for her, Vanitha recollected. There was no let up and the punishments were an on going regular affair. There was hardly any part of her body that had not received his brutal attention. Anything and everything was sufficient reason for him to get provoked and harass the wife....the dosa went cold, her posture was wrong when the guest turned in, she smiled an ounce more than that was required in presence of his friends, failed to open the gate at the right time and so on. Her ear drums were damaged and she had perpetual stomach pain as a result of being kicked around. Vanitha is all thankful to God since her husband took her to the ENT specialist when infection became worse in the ear and got the eardrum replaced through surgery. Her husband took special attention to see that she doesn't speak to their friends except in his presence. Further her husband had the phone disconnected thus effectively cutting her access to the outside world. She became a total slave to her husband in every sense...minimum communication...strict obeyance of all his demands, some of which crossed all human considerations...sexual perversions ...limited food....no clothing....no outing ....she felt she was in an altogether different world. But as Vanitha recalls her little sweetheart's cute face and looks were more than enough for her to forget everything and survive somehow.

During the next two years, Vanitha underwent three forced MTPs for fear of life of her child and herself. Starting with insults, proceeding on to abuse and ending up with physical tortures he would succeed in making Vanitha agree with the MTP. Vanitha suffered all this in silence for she was really afraid that in a fit of anger her husband might even murder her and the baby girl. The reason attributed for each abortion was just the same.... 'you can't give birth to a male baby'. Her graduate mother in law somehow succeeded in making the son and the rest of the family believe her new theory that Vanitha is no longer going to mother a son. According to her, Vanitha's small belly of the previous time definitely indicated a boy baby but Vanitha with her deep likeness for a girl baby and daily prayers could change the sex of the child. Vanitha's pleas to give her a second chance ended up in further tortures. Today Vanitha recollects how much she longed for a companion to her only daughter.

The night before each abortion she had the same unique dream. During a school trip to Kanyakumari, when she was eight years old, the children were assembled on the sea shore to witness the beautiful sunset. But instead of enjoying the sunset, the little girl was frightened of the ferocious waves and the darkly outlined rocks that were spread along the shore taking the brunt of the onslaught of the incoming waves. The sinister shaped rocks frightened her no end. Vanitha imagined being alone on top of one of the rocks and crying out loudly to her mother for help. Some how or other this was etched in her unconscious mind. The fright and terror she felt in her childhood remained with her. This nightmare on the eve of each forced abortion was traumatic. She felt like a lonely and helpless child calling out to her mother for help! Or was it the thoughts about the helplessness of an unborn foetus that put her into such a dream..... still now she is not sure. After each abortion she was rushed away from the hospital without her being given the required bed rest. To avoid curious eyes, her husband forced Vanitha to travel on a speeding bike in her dazed condition, clinging for dear life. She had no choice at all. What gave her the necessary courage was that she was going to see her little princess. Any hesitation on her part invited another bout of abuse from her husband and an equally callous mother-in-law.

By a quirk of fate, the third abortion was in her native place and by far her worst shock. She had gone home to visit her ailing mother who soon passed away. Though she knew she was pregnant she kept it a secret. However she could not keep her secret for long. One day while she was at her husband's home, the smell of the special curry prepared by her mother-in-law, forced the bile in her stomach to come up and Vanitha had to rush out to avoid making a mess by vomiting all over. The sister-in-law, who had hitherto ignored her, was eagerness personified and rushed her to the nearby hospital for confirmation of pregnancy. The positive result and her refusal to undergo yet another abortion brought her non-stop harassment and threats from her husband's mother and sisters alike during the next two days. The husband, who arrived from Bhopal hearing the confirmation of pregnancy, literally dragged her to the hospital. Her heart rendering pleas for mercy fell on the deaf years of the medical staff, four of whom, held her down in the operation theatre to do the D&C stating that since they had already accepted the payment they were unable to help her.

But what shocked and humiliated her most, even in her semi-conscious condition, was the doctor's observation that the frequent D&Cs had left her uterus scarred so thoroughly. The doctor stated further that if she had known this earlier, she would not have consented to doing a D&C. Within an hour she was back home where contempt and anger of her in laws awaited her. Towards evening Vanitha became sick with heavy bleeding, fever and shivering. Nobody except her daughter cared for her. The little girl sat beside her mother without knowing why and how her mother has become sick, soothening her with all sweet words, and caressing her with the little fingers. Towards night, the young one happened to pick up the phone while others were chatting in the courtyard. It was Vanitha's brother on the other end to whom she conveyed the mother's illness and how she was trembling with fever and cannot even speak.

It was her brother's timely intervention that brought Vanitha back to life. On the way to parental home, she was taken to the same doctor who did the D&C who took pity on her and gave her necessary injection to stop the severe bleeding. She was hospitalised for three days in her native place. She recollected how her husband remained cool and indifferent while the brother rushed in and took Vanitha to parental home, how much she wished for the presence and company of her husband even at that sinking stage and how cruel he was in not accompanying them to the hospital in his city which was not familiar to Vanitha and her brother.

The outcome of the last forced visit to the hospital made Vanitha sit back and take stock of her situation. The three days in the hospital bed gave Vanitha enough time to take certain firm decisions. She could sense how worthless her life has become, how she is treated as a sex object by her husband, how she has lost all control on her own thinking and her own body, how she is locked up without an outlet for her feelings and desires, how she is totally dependent on a cruel and selfish husband. Vanitha decided that a stop had to be put to all this.....not to be a slave of her husband and in laws any more. She started looking within .....is there anything worthy in her... any powers or skills. The search didn't last long because she had such an excellent track record in her studies... the class topper ...the favourite of all her teachers...the merit scholarship winner. She decided to study further and secure a decent job so as to become independent first.

She realized that in the name of tradition and accepted family values, she had allowed her husband and his family to ruin her life. She also thought of the many others sailing in the same boat like her. Sacrificing personal freedom and happiness, blindly obeying the elders of the family and husbands was in effect the undoing of the women paving the way for their miserable existence. Though the Union Government had enacted the PNDT Act in 1994, it had not prevented her husband and for that matter the medics, in forcing her to undergo an MTP in 1995!

Years passed by and now Vanitha has become such a powerful woman that she is successfully changing the miserable lives of hundreds and thousands of unfortunate fellow women.

When I encouraged her to share her success stories she started unfolding them one by one. Being an academically brilliant person, she set out to alleviate her own sufferings first by going in for higher studies in the required disciplines. She had to face lot of challenges and protests from her own people and husband's family when she stepped out to study further. According to them it was not fair for a married girl and especially a mother from an aristocratic family to go for studies. But her hard work was well paid, she came out with flying colours in the examinations. Immediately she got a prestigious job opportunity and according to Vanitha she never had to look back. Even her husband was shocked to see the way she was excelling in her studies and her career. She was no more a dependent and she started enjoying freedom and security, not the kind of security from marriage for which girls will have to pay a high price but the one derived from her own earnings and which made her feel proud of herself. In Vanitha's own version a post graduate degree and a heavy package of dowry couldn't earn her any dignity in her husband's home. When she failed to produce a son for the family, she was crushed like a doormat not only by the husband but also by the in laws. But when she became economically independent, on one side she got the courage to fight for a dignified life and on the other side love and respect naturally started flowing in from all directions.

Later she decided to use her freshly acquired skills to kick start the spreading of an awareness campaign in the community for the sake of emancipation of all women. Her being mobbed at the seminar is proof enough of the inroads she has made since then. Her plans for the future was enlightening and motivating for me as an academician in Women's Studies. According to Vanitha, no woman should suffer in silence like her to make her husband and his family happy by blindly taking orders and obeying. Struggles in her life have tought Vanitha that overcoming the social and cultural barriers, which often prevent women from reacting to the injustices being inflicted on them, was a tall order. She is all set to direct her energies, her education and all skills at her command to bring about the necessary change in women's lives.

When we finally said good night around 2 AM, I couldn't but blurt out the one question that was upper most in mind – are you still married to him and do you still love him? Her calm and quiet answer was in the affirmative – "I am still married to him and I love him". Looking into my inquisitive eyes she explained, "As I went from strength to strength in my mission, I realized his weakness. He was a victim of tradition, the bad influence of his mother, father and elders weighed heavily in making him what he is. No one is perfect and if the negative socialization and its internalisation is so strong what can one do?" She went on how her husband's family boasts about the grandfather's aversion to girl children. Years back when grandmother delivered a daughter after the birth of five sons, the grandfather went inside the room, had a look at the girl baby ... made a spitting sound and came out in fury to the veranda. Vanitha remembers how often this story is repeated in the get togethers of the family as if the grandfather has done a great deal. She asked me, "what else can you expect of a grandson when a daughter is born to him?" I nodded in agreement. "Taking time I analyzed his problems, the flaw in his personality and found solutions. He accepted them reluctantly and by dint of hard work and persuasion I won him over to my side. Thank God for his blessings".

Today Vanitha's husband is a pro-feminist who does not want to be reminded of the past. He has even expressed his regret for having got himself sterilized in the sixth year of marriage as an act of revenge to prevent further pregnancies. 'When I see him suffering in silence looking over families with two or more children, I pity today's young couples who wish for only one child not realizing the difficulties in bringing up their only one issue without companionship', added Vanitha. 'And, definitely not knowing what the future holds out'. There have been changes in the home front too. The in-laws have come closer. Vanitha is respected and looked up to by her husband's family. Her daughter, once neglected and cursed, is the darling of the house.

My final question to Vanitha was had she informed her parents of her predicament in Bhopal would they not have come to her rescue? Probably this in turn might have given her a different life altogether. She answered truthfully enough that if she had informed them, they would have died of a heart attack soon. According to tradition, once a girl is given away in marriage, the parents' duty is over. Whatever happens to her thereafter, she has to accept it with a pinch of salt. After marriage a daughter is just a guest in her own family where she grew up – a visitor who stays for a short duration. An extended stay for whatever reason is not welcome and will upset the household The life's vagaries are for her to suffer alone and not to be passed on to her family. In Vanitha's version if she had informed her parents about her fate in Bhopal, she definitely would have lost her parents, her husband and the family relationships. But today she has won her husband and his family and both families take pride in her achievements.

Vanitha's sacrifices in silence and the realization that it all had gone in vain, gave Vanitha the strength to resurrect her life and point herself in the right direction. Her new found freedom and innumerable assignments keep her quite busy leaving no time to brood. ***Vanitha is making useful contributions for the betterment of life all around and she is now looked upon as a role model and leader for hundreds of girls and women who need leaders who will lead not from the power of their positions, but from the power that comes from living exemplary lives and who lead by their own examples.***

Today we put our combined resources to work for the betterment of not women alone but the families as a whole for:

A WOMAN HAS EXTRA ORDINARY STRENGTH TO STOP THE BUCK AND SPIN A SAFETY WEB AROUND HERSELF AND HER NEAR AND DEAR ONES. LET US NOT FORGET THAT WOMEN CAN BRING UP RESPONSIBLE AND RESPONSIVE CITIZENS OF GENERATION NEXT. THE ONLY THING IS WOMAN NEEDS TO BE REMINDED OF HER STRENGTH AND GIVEN THE SPACE TO LIVE AND GROW. A PLEDGE TO SUPPORT THEM IS TIMELY AND A MUST. SO LET US GO TO IT.............................

2

Are Baby Girls Children of a Lesser God?

"Women have been the mere echoes of men. Our laws and constitutions, our creeds and codes, and the customs of social life are all of masculine origin. The true woman is as yet a dream of the future" (Elizabeth Cady Stanton, 1998). Contextually at present we live in an altogether different world with the Feminist Movement, Socialism, the United Nations Charter for the Equal Rights for Men and Women, the Universal Declaration of Human Rights and our own Constitution with its Fundamental rights. Unlimited laws have been enacted for women today. Interestingly they reflect the two sides of the same coin. They show that we live in a progressive society which wants to do away with the 'old skins' of our past's way of thinking and doing and is also proof of the cruelties and atrocities which were and are rampant even now.

Jawaharlal Nehru, the first prime minister of independent India opined, "You can tell the condition of a nation by looking at the status of its women". Women's quest for equality with men has become universal. Barring a few exceptions and some bright patches here and there, where some women have become known and conspicuous, the rest remain victims of negligence, exploitation, harassment and atrocities. Millions of women throughout the world live in conditions of abject deprivation and attacks against their fundamental human rights for no other reason than they are women. The existence of gender bias, male domination and female subjugation can be traced back to the old Roman days where a man was accepted as the ultimate owner of his wife/wives, children and slaves.

It is commonly accepted that we acquire our initial identity as men and women through self-evident biological characteristics. But it is not often realized that these biological differences get translated into another set of identities, which have profound implications for the way life is lived by women and men. Gender is the social construction, which refers to what society deems appropriate in terms of one's behavior, roles, attitudes, opportunities and command over resources. There are important differences in the quality of life, amount of work done, health, literacy levels, economic, political and social standing of males and females. Women make up 50% of the world's population, comprise 33.3% of labour force, perform nearly 66.6% of all working hours, receive 10% of the world's income and own less than 1% of world's property. Discrimination and exploitation on the basis of gender constitutes a serious issue. It effectively means that half the human race is unable to realize its potential and condemned to sub-optional standards of existence.

Patriarchy controls women's productive or labour power, women's reproduction, women's sexuality, women's mobility and women's access to property and other economic resources. Since such a control takes the form of paternalistic dominance whereby women are provided with food, shelter and security amidst outsiders and strict obedience is demanded in return out of mutual obligation, it becomes difficult to recognize and fight against male control. Patriarchal ideology is perpetuated by the various social institutions like family, religion, law, and media, political, educational and economic institutions, which act as pillars of a patriarchal structure making it natural and invincible.

One of the most serious impediments to women's development is the phenomenon of continuing and increasing violence against them. Violence against women is one of the most significant, yet little understood and acknowledged factors instrumental in the phenomenon of marginalization of women in the development process. Gender violence manifests itself in various forms such as female foeticide and infanticide, eve-teasing, sexual abuse, incest, molestation, sexual harassment at work place and on the streets, marital rape, dowry deaths, forced pregnancy, wife-beating, mental torture etc.

We all believe that a woman gives wholeness to the family, but hardly have we ever contemplated over the wholeness of a woman, the desires and dreams she holds. The patriarchal society at large considers women as the second class citizens and it is for this reason that the liberty and existence of women are trodden most of the times. Today, though our society has undergone a drastic change in several aspects, no change has occurred so far as the victimization of a woman is concerned. A woman has been suffering and struggling for her very birthrights. Gender inequality in health care, nutrition, education, female foeticide and infanticide, substance abuse, early marriage, teenage pregnancy, unwed mothers, prostitution, sexual abuse, environmental deprivation and disparities in rights fulfillment are on the rise in the modern families and societies.

"A daughter is born, it's a howling disgrace
Misery and pain is written large on her face.

The in-laws are wild, at the female child.
The neighbours come to mourn
That a girl, alas! is born.
They groan and they cry
Start worrying about her marriage.
And prepare to bid her good bye".
(Jyoti Mhapsekar)

While a son is considered an asset, a daughter is considered a liability. There is a proverb, 'Bringing up a girl is like watering a plant in the neighbour's garden'. To some extent, the neglect and abuse of female foetuses, infants and children is a phenomenon common to several cultures.

Unequal Status of Women in India

India with a population of more than one billion is the world's second most populous country. Of that number, 120 million are women who live in poverty. In India male domination with a complementary suppression of women has been continuing since pre historic times. It is a stark reality, that the life of an average Indian woman is still governed by customs, habits, prejudices and unwritten codes of conduct. The violation of the rights of women is a human rights violation. A family is considered as the abode of tender feelings and relationships. It is within the four walls of family, the root of all culture, that the discrimination against women starts. Women comprise nearly 50% of India's population and still they continue to be treated most unfairly and unjustly in almost all walks of life. The position of women in India has taken a severe beating over the last few years. It is a grave irony that on one side women in India are charting the path of success along with their male counterparts hand in hand, while simultaneously they are being subjected to all kinds of physical and mental abuse. Statistics reveals that in India every 26 minutes a woman is molested and every 42 minutes a sexual harassment incident occurs and every 34 minutes a rape takes place.

In Indian society the status of women has changed from time to time; position of women in society is the index to the standard of social organization. Sex composition of human population is one of the basic demographic characteristics, which is extremely vital for any meaningful demographic analysis. Changes in sex composition largely reflect the underlying socio economic and cultural patterns of the society. Sex ratio is an indication of the extent of prevailing equality between males and females at a given time. It has been estimated that around the year 2000, the world had 986 females against 1000 males whereas in India it was only 933 females per 1000 males. India is one of the few countries where males significantly outnumber females, and this imbalance has increased over time. It is estimated that deaths of young girls in India exceed those of young boys over 300,000 each year, and every sixth infant death is specifically due to gender discrimination. Of the 15 million baby girls born in India each year, nearly 25 percent will not live to see their 15th birthday.

The Indian constitution grants women equal rights with men, but strong patriarchal traditions persist, with women's lives shaped by customs that are centuries old. In most Indian families, a daughter is viewed as a liability, and she is conditioned to believe that she is inferior and subordinate to men. Sons are idolized and celebrated. *'May you be the mother of a hundred sons'* is a common Hindu wedding blessing. In India there has been a continuous decline in the sex ratio since 1901 to 1981 from 972 women per 1000 men to 934 women per 1000 men respectively. In 1991 it became the lowest in the history of the Census with a count of 927 women per 1000 men. In 2001, the sex ratio again became 933 per 1000.

There are numerous accounts of the prevalence of strategies for discrimination against girl children. This has ranged from female infanticide (Venkatachalam and Srinivasan, 1993; Chunkath and Athreya, 1997; George, 1997) to care and food related deprivation. Further there is evidence to suggest that excess female infant mortality significantly contributes to the overall decline in the sex ratio in India (Miller, 1981; Sudha and Rajan, 1999; Census of India, 2001). Among the major nations of the world, India is the only exception that shows a regular decline in sex ratio over the last century as shown in Table 1.

TABLE 1
Sex Ratio in India 1901 – 2001

Census Year	*Sex Ratio Females / 1000 Males*
1901	972
1911	964
1921	955
1931	950
1941	945
1951	946
1961	941
1971	930
1981	934
1991	927
2001	933

Source: Census 2001.

The deficit of women as per sex ratio statistics reveals an alarming rise from 3 million in 1901 to 36 million in 2001. This trend has given rise to the concept of 'missing girls' as connoted by the Nobel Laureate Amartya Sen. "Given a preference for boys over girls that may manifest itself in the form of the parents wanting the newborn to be a boy rather than a girl. There was a time when this would be no more than a wish, but with the availability of modern techniques to determine the gender of the foetus, sex-selective abortion has become common in many countries. This is high-tech sexism" (Sen, 2001).

There are reasons to believe that it is increasingly becoming a common practice across the country to determine the sex of the unborn child or foetus and eliminate it if the foetus is found to be a female. This practice is referred to as pre-birth elimination of females (PBEF). PBEF involves two stages: determination of sex of the foetus and induced termination if the foetus is not of the desired sex. This practice widely termed, as female foeticide is believed to be one of the significant contributors to the adverse child sex ratio in India.

The declining trend in sex ratio is seen in almost all the states of the country. The major states that are largely responsible for decline are Punjab, Uttar Pradesh, Bihar, Orissa, Jharkand, Chattisgarh, Madhya Pradesh, Gujarat, Maharashtra and Tamil Nadu. Reasons like neglect of girl child resulting in their higher mortality at younger ages, high maternal mortality, female infanticide, female foeticide etc. are considered to be responsible for the low level of sex ratio. The sharp decline in sex ratio is a matter of grave concern as it is expected to lead to serious demographic imbalances and social consequences. Female foeticide is a gross violation of many rights; namely the right of a female child to be born, right of a woman to take decisions about her health and pregnancy, and access to safe, effective, affordable and acceptable methods of family planning and the right to a safe pregnancy, child birth and a healthy infant.

Traditional son preference is particularly widespread in China, North Korea, India and Pakistan. In China and India sons enjoy a great deal of social prestige than daughters. The family name is passed down through sons, who are also financially responsible for supporting their parents during old age. In India, a precept of the Hindu religion holds that a sonless father cannot achieve salvation and male children can only perform a significant Hindu funeral rite for their fathers. The most striking determinant of son preference in India is the dowry system. In the last two decades fuelled by a consumer boom, dowry has spread like an epidemic to communities that never practiced it before whereby girl child is considered a liability rather than an asset. Women are socially conditioned to accept that unless they produce one or more sons they have no social worth.

Son preference has been prevalent in the Indian society since ages. Modernization has not undermined male preference, instead by raising the costs of having a daughter, from needing to educate her to greater demands at the time of marriage, it has reinforced it. When patriarchal ideologies meet up with ideologies of development, which, on the one hand, marginalize women and, on the other, are based on population control (emanating from the 'population bomb' theory) and use modern technology as their handmaidens, the very existence of the girl child is threatened.

Advances in medical technology have made sex determination easily accessible to the masses whereby female foeticide has become a common evil. Amniocentesis, Chorionic Villous Biopsy, Sonography, Ultrasound Scanning, Imaging Techniques etc. are used for prenatal diagnosis and subsequent abortion of the female foetus. This easy access to sex determination technology has led to the sharp decline in child sex ratio (0-6 years) in almost all the prosperous states of Punjab, Haryana, Himachal Pradesh, Gujarat and Delhi. Various studies have shown that relative prosperity has enabled the use of advanced scientific technology to do away with girls before they are born (Jain, 1985; Kusum, 1993; Sen, 2001; Patel, 2003).

Several studies have documented the discriminatory practice of son preference especially in the northern and central states of the country (Subrata, 1974; Muthurayappa et al., 1997; Arnold et al., 1998; Arokiasamy, 2002). The NFHS II (1998-99) results show a preference for sons over daughters in all the southern states at varying degrees as given in Table 2.

TABLE 2
Number of Sons or Daughters Wanted by Women

States	Mean Ideal Number of Sons	Mean Ideal Number of Daughters	Want More (%) Sons	Want More (%) Daughters	Want at least 1% Sons	Want at least 1% Daughters
Andhra Pradesh	1.0	0.8	19.8	2.7	76.0	71.3
Karnataka	0.9	0.5	13.0	1.9	70.0	67.5
Kerala	1.0	0.8	14.6	5.2	72.6	70.7
Tamil Nadu	0.8	0.7	9.6	1.9	66.3	63.9

Source: National Family Health Survey (NFHS – 11), 1998 - 99.

Table 2 shows that among the southern states Kerala stands next to Andhra Pradesh in its son preference. The findings such as the mean ideal number of sons and daughters wanted in the families, the percentage of families preferring more sons than daughters or more daughters than sons, percentage of families desiring at least one son and one daughter showed that the families valued sons more than the daughters. Further analysis of the data regarding sex preference of ever married women by State, 1998-99 reveals that in India, the mean ideal number of sons and daughters are lowest among the southern states along with Goa. The point that deserves utmost concern with regard to the present study is that Kerala has the lowest fertility rate and its society strictly adheres to small family norms. Here the preference and obsession for son has every chance to urge people adopt sex selection techniques including prenatal diagnosis and subsequent female foeticide.

Sex Ratio of Kerala

Kerala is the only state in the country, which shows a fairly good sex ratio in favor of women. The god's own country with its high human development indices comparable to those of the developed West occupies the status of a model state as far as women development is concerned. Kerala's reproductive health indices such as low maternal mortality rate, low infant mortality rate and low fertility rate are comparable to that of the developed West. Besides the cent percent literacy rate and high educational standards make the society an elite one among the rest of the states. The overall sex ratio during 1991 and 2001 for the whole country and for the state of Kerala prima-facie testifies the existence of a favourable socio-cultural milieu for women in Kerala.

India	*1991*	*2001*
	927	933
Kerala	1036	1058

Source: Census of India 2001.

The causal variables attributed to this fair sex ratio are the high level of women's literacy, more access for women to well paid and well respected jobs, low fertility rate of 1.7 children per couple, openness to and interaction with the outside world and the activist left-wing politics which fights strongly on issues of equality.

Further analysis of Census 2001 especially of **the age-wise data of Kerala population (given as Appendix 1)** reveals some shocking facts with regard to the actual condition in the state. There are debates about whether Kerala is gradually inclining towards the national scenario where there is increased male bias. As per the Census details of Kerala, in the 0-6 age group, the sex ratio was 963 and the total 0-6 age group population was 36.5 lakhs. Out of this 18.6 lakhs were male babies and infants and 17.9 lakhs were female babies and infants. Life expectancy of women in Kerala is 73 years which is greater than that of men at 67. In Kerala about 11% of the population is in the 60+ category and there are 1120 females to 1000 men in this category. The unfair masculinisation of the young and feminization of the old is clarified by Figure 1.

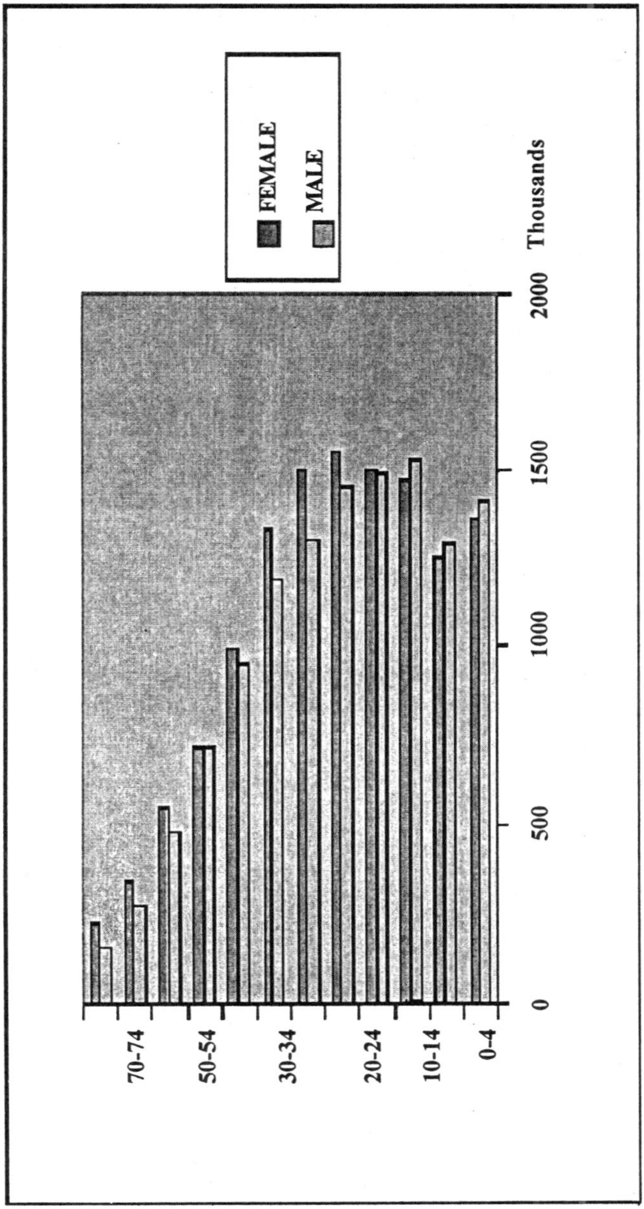

Source: Census of India 2001.

FIGURE 1 Age-wise Kerala Population

Figure 1 shows a higher concentration of females towards the upper age group and a declining trend in the lower age groups. There are debates about whether Kerala is gradually inclining towards the national scenario where there is increased male bias or whether this is a natural biological phenomenon, which evens out when we look at sex ratio from age 10 onwards.

In Kerala gender gaps are not explicit. Careful scrutiny and probing into the subtle patriarchal forces and dynamics that repress women would shed light on the real picture of women's status and the discrimination they suffer from. As such a scrutiny of the favorably placed sex ratio of Census 2001 reveals that in all the 14 districts of Kerala except Wayanad and Idukki, the overall sex ratio favors women but the child sex ratio particularly in the 0–6 age group shows an anti–women trend. Boys outnumber girls in all the districts including Wayanad and Idukki. **The overall sex ratio and child sex ratio in various districts of Kerala as per Census 2001 is given as Appendix II.**

Kerala has the lowest proportion of children in all the three age groups of 10-14, 5-9 and 0-4 among the states of India. The lowest proportion of female children 0-4 years old is also in Kerala. The lowest fertility rate along with lowest number of children without a corresponding decline in the number of boys 0-4 years is a matter of serious concern. Doesn't it indicate a negative attitude towards the girl child and an undue son preference of the whole state? As per Table 3, a comparison of the child sex ratio with the overall sex ratio of Kerala reveals a wide gender gap, which in turn is higher than the comparative gender gap observed in the prosperous northern states with widespread use of sex determination tests.

What might be the factors that have led to this masculinisation of Kerala society especially during the last one decade? Doesn't it imply a selection of the desirable and rejection

TABLE 3
Sex Ratios in States with Widespread Use of Sex Determination Tests along with that of Kerala

State	*Child Sex Ratio*	*Overall Sex Ratio*	*Sex Ratio Deficit in Child Group*
Punjab	793	857	64
Haryana	820	861	41
Gujarat	878	921	43
Maharashtra	917	922	5
Kerala	963	1058	95

Source: Census of India 2001.

of the undesirable? We have the PNDT Act enacted in 1994 and amended in 2003. But an impact of sex selective abortion is seen in terms of the widening gender gap among 0-6 age group. Easy access to the NRT's such as foetoscopy, ultrasonography, chorione villous biopsy, foetal blood sampling and the latest sperm selection techniques might have tempted the so called educated and elite citizens of Kerala, resort to pre-natal sex determination and elimination of the female foetus.

It was in this instance that the present study was undertaken to investigate whether son preference exists among Keralites, which may indirectly lead to sex selective abortions accounting for missing girls. Facts from states like Punjab, Hariyana, Chandigarh and Delhi, which have the lowest sex ratios in the country, underline the direct link between son preference, sex selective abortions and low sex ratios.

The index of son preference during 1990 in Kerala was only 11.7 with 12th position when the country average was 20. In Tamil Nadu with 13th position the index was 9.2. The lowest proportion of female children 0-4 years old was in Kerala and Tamil Nadu as per the latest Census reports. It was in these circumstances that an independent project on "MISSING GIRLS IN KERALA: THE BACKLASH OF SON PREFERENCE" was taken up by the author with a view to unravel the reasons that have led to a declining trend especially of the 'second sex'.

The term 'Missing Girls' is conceived as the number of girls in the age group of 0-6 years who are expected to be present in the population as per demographic norms of Kerala but is found to be deficit as per Census 2001 details.

The study has been designed to attain the following objectives:

1. To find out whether son preference exists in Kerala society as per the total sample and the sub samples formed on the basis of gender, locale, religion, education and income levels.

2. To find out whether there will be a significant association between the responses to existence of son preference in Kerala society and the classificatory variables viz. gender, locale, religion, education and income levels.

3. To compare the attitude towards female foeticide, of people belonging to the two districts of Ernakulam and Malappuram for the total sample and the sub samples formed on the basis of gender, locale, religion, education and income levels.

4. To analyze the major reasons responsible for son preference in Kerala society as per the total sample and the sub samples formed on the basis of gender, locale, religion, education and income levels.

5. To suggest measures for the prevention of discriminatory practices like son preference and female foeticide.

3

The Perils of Gender Discrimination

"In the chequered history of mankind one finds that different and disparate cultures, however distant they may be in time and space, have at least one thing in common and that is the contempt for women" (Siddiqui & Ranganathan, 2001). The unequal status of women though offensive to human dignity and violative of human rights has evolved as a stumbling block to human development the world over. Women as a group is often oppressed, exploited and disadvantaged people among others like the poor, the lower castes and people from the backward regions.

The gender differentiating ideology is frequently identified only at the level of the gender system's impact on women. The impact pertains to the manifestation of gender ideology in women's illiteracy, exploitation, economic dependence, early marriage, wife beating, and dowry demands etc. The invisible aspects of the ideology remain hidden and unnoticed beneath the visible aspects. Stereotyped roles, lack of access to productive education and jobs, gender oppressive practices like son preference, restricted social mobility, and dowry exchange are the more visible manifestations of the gender differentiating system of patriarchy. It is patriarchy that provides the life force to the unfavorable conditions that women face (Dagar, 1998). The gender difference and bias, perceived as existing globally, place women all over the world at various disadvantageous positions.

In most societies women are expected to be passive, obedient, caring and nurturing whereas men are expected to be strong, active, adventurous and rational. While men are considered to be the heads of households, bread-winners, owners and managers of property, and active in politics, religion, business and the professions, women are expected and trained to bear and look after children, to nurse the infirm and old, do all household work and so on (Bhasin, 2004). At every stage of life and in every sphere of social living a woman has to face a multitude of discriminatory practices. The socialization process at home instills the learned helplessness in girls, which get strengthened and deepened with time by other agencies of socialization. In matters of literacy and education, the rates of enrolment and retention at schools are different for boys and girls. In aspects related to health and nutrition, girls and women are the last and least fed. When it comes to employment, women are the last to be hired and first to be fired. In the labour market males command the majority of jobs with high prestige, high skill and high income and this is true throughout the industrial world. Even now equal pay for equal work is not the norm in most countries.

In the workplace a woman has to do double the work than that of a man in order to get acceptance. Men are better educated and better trained and they do not have to carry the double burden of work whereupon their professional graphs rise much higher than that of women. The dual role conflicts resulting from gender division of labour especially within the families is quite a de-motivating factor for working women. Still women as a group constitute an important part of labour force of the

Indian economy. Women work longer hours and contribute more than men in terms of total labour energy spent by the family members. But their work most often remains invisible, unrecognized and unpaid or under paid. Such discriminations account for the UN statistics like "women do more than 60 percent of the hours of work done in the world, but they get 10 percent of the world's income and own one percent of the world's property" (Human Development Report, 2001).

Gender injustice taking the shape of crimes against women has escalated all over the world and India is no exception to this. In spite of the constitutional and legal provisions aimed at ensuring gender equality, positive judicial trends, welfare schemes and activism of feminist groups, women continue to suffer from violence both in and outside homes. As per the records of National Crime Records Bureau, Government of India (2001), every hour there is one case of sexual harassment, one dowry death, two rapes, four molestations and six cases of cruelty by husband and his relatives.

The gender discrimination in the four major areas of education, skills, health and employment has been summarized by Dagar (1998) as follows:

SPHERE	*TYPES OF DISCRIMINATION*
Education	Girls may be sent to local/regional schools rather than model/English medium schools where their brothers may be studying. Girls may not be sent regularly to school.
Skills	Girls may be encouraged to acquire home-oriented skills with little market value (home science, cooking, social science)
Health	Girls may be given inferior nutritional intake. Differential material care for female and male children.

(Contd.)

(Contd. Table)

SPHERE	*TYPES OF DISCRIMINATION*
	Females may be treated by hakims/quacks. Medical attention may be delayed in case of females
Employment	Soft jobs even in professions (female I.A.S as social welfare cultural secretaries, MBAs in personal department etc.)
	Wage and technology differentiation (for instance in Ludhiana, female hosiery workers work on Indian machinery with 1/5 of the productivity of the Japanese machines on which males work.) Females may be largely contractual and unorganized sector workers.

According to Sen (2001), inequality between men and women is one of the crucial disparities in many societies. This is reflected not only in such fields as education and opportunity to develop talents but also in more elementary fields of nutrition, health and survival. Also the afflicted world in which we live is characterized by deeply unequal sharing of the burden of adversities between women and men. Sen identifies the following seven types of inequality that exist in most parts of the world:

1. Mortality Inequality: There is an unusually high mortality rate of women in societies with gender bias in health care and nutrition. Mortality inequality has been observed extensively in North Africa and in Asia, including China and South Asia.

2. Natality Inequality: With a preference for boys over girls and with the availability of modern techniques to determine the gender of the foetus, sex selective abortion (high- tech sexism) has become common in many countries. It is particularly prevalent in East Asia, in China and South Korea in particular, but also in Singapore and

Taiwan, and it is beginning to emerge as a statistically significant phenomenon in India and South Asia as well.

3. Basic Facility Inequality: There are many countries in Asia and Africa, and also in Latin America, where girls have far less opportunity of schooling than boys do. There are other deficiencies in basic facilities available to women, varying from encouragement to cultivate one's natural talents to fair participation in rewarding social functions of the community.

4. Special Opportunity Inequality: Even when there is relatively little difference in basic facilities including schooling, the opportunities of higher education may be far fewer for young women than for young men. Gender bias in higher education and professional training can be observed in some of the richest countries in the world, in Europe and North America.

5. Professional Inequality: In terms of employment as well as promotion in work and occupation, women often face greater handicap than men. A country like Japan may be quite egalitarian in matters of demography or basic facilities, and even to a great extent, in higher education, and yet progress to elevated levels of employment and occupation seems to be much more problematic for women than for men.

6. Ownership Inequality: In many societies the ownership of property can also be very unequal. Even basic assets such as homes and land may be very asymmetrically shared. The absence of claims to property can not only reduce the voice of women but also make it harder for women to enter and flourish in commercial, economic and even some social activities.

7. Household Inequality: There are often basic inequalities in gender relations within the family or the household,

which can take many different forms. The family arrangements can be quite unequal in terms of sharing the burden of housework and child care. In many societies while men will naturally work outside the home, women could do it if and only if they could combine it with various inescapable and unequally shared household duties. The reach of this inequality includes not only unequal relations within the family, but also derivative inequalities in employment and recognition in the outside world.

The seven types of inequalities can impose diverse adversities on the lives of not only women and girls but also those of men and boys through biological connections and societal connections. According to Sen, since gender inequalities take different forms and very often feed each other establishing strong interlinkages, it is very difficult to put an end to this evil practice.

History of Son Preference and Female Foeticide in India

India's total population on 1st March 2001 stood at 1.03 billion persons. With this, India became the second country in the world, after China, to cross the one billion mark. The population of the country rose by 21.34 % between 1991 and 2001.What did not rise, but rather declined shockingly was the child sex ratio. The child sex ratio is calculated as number of girls per 1000 boys in the 0-6 age group. In India, however, the 1991 Census reported a child sex ratio of 945 girls per 1000 boys which further declined to 927 during 2001 Census.

An obsession with sons from the age of Adharwa Veda exists in India, the land famous for its enduring values. It is given in the Vedas "Let a female child be born somewhere else. Here let a son be born". The son preference further got legitimized by the law giver Manu's treatise and strengthened through tradition and belief has percolated down to 21st century India. According to demographic calculations more than 90 million women are missing, worldwide. The traditional preference for sons is deeply rooted in the cultural traditions of the society. This discriminatory preference is widespread in China, North Korea, India and Pakistan. The son preference is influenced by many socio-economic and cultural factors such as the son being responsible for carrying forward the family name, contributing to family income, being considered as a source of support during old age, of religious rites at the time of cremation, practice of dowry and the daughters being viewed as "paraya dhan". In agricultural households due to rivalries and animosity resulting from land disputes male offsprings are considered as a source of power.

Son preference affects women in many countries, particularly in Asia. Its consequences can be anything from foetal or female infanticide to neglect of the girl child over her brother when it comes to essential needs such as nutrition, health care and education. In China and India, some women choose to terminate their pregnancies when expecting daughters but carry their pregnancies to term when expecting sons. Girls are exterminated at the time of conception itself. The abhorrent practice of female foeticide is a gross violation of natural laws and women's basic rights.

Though abortions are legally permissible in the country, most of the MTPs today are contributing towards female foeticide. Due to the advances in technology, determining the sex of the foetus in the womb at a very early stage is possible now. The technology revolution in medical research offered pre-birth sex selection techniques such as amniocentesis, ultrasound and scan machines, chorine villous biopsy, and the latest sperm selection techniques to exterminate the unwanted sex.

Today all pregnant women who could afford it are being routinely referred for ultrasounds in early pregnancy, to be on the safe side. These new technologies were initially intended to help the detection of foetal abnormalities and application of the necessary therapy, wherever possible, at the appropriate time. But today these have been used not only to detect the sex of the foetus but also to opt for abortion of a female foetus. This practice is worse than female infanticide in the sense that the violation of justice does not even become visible. The practice of prenatal sex determination and female foeticide is not confined to the uneducated or poorer sections of the society but is more rampant among the educated and seemingly modern rich people. A study of amniocentesis procedures conducted in a large Bombay hospital found that 95.5 percent of foetuses identified as female were aborted compared with a far smaller percentage of male foetuses.

Techniques of Prenatal Sex Determination

There are various technologies and methods for preconceptional sex selection and post conceptional sex detection such as amniocentesis, chorionic villi sampling or biopsy, ultrasound imaging, foetoscopy, alpha-foetoprotein measurement and maternal serum screening. The most important among these are briefly described below:

(a) Preconceptional Sex Selection

1. Shettles Method

It is a sperm selection technique, which takes account of the different characteristics of the androgenic and gynogenic sperms. This facilitates the desired pairing if carefully linked with the timing of ovulation and a favourable environment in the vagina, produced with an alkaline or acidic douche (Parikh, 1989). Another is to separate sperm cells into male and female cells and afterwards to inseminate artificially with sperm of desired choice. One way to achieve this result is by marking the Y- (male chromosomes) with a fluorescent colour. Thereafter, with a laser beam, sperm cells are sorted out one by one in cell – sorter. It is a very expensive method as the apparatus costs around a million Dutch guilders.

2. Ericsson Method

This method named after its discoverer, the American reproductive physiologist, Ronald Ericsson is a more commonly used technique to spin the sperm through a protein-based gel. Y-Chromosome bearing sperm cells are lighter and tend to swim faster to the top; X-female chromosome bearing sperm cells, are heavier, and sink to the bottom. By inseminating women with sperm, which has been selected in this manner the conception of a child of a desired sex, is sought. This procedure is said to improve the chance up to 75 per cent (normally it would be 50 per cent). Dr. Gita Pandya, of India's Foundation for Research in Reproduction in Bombay, is a franchise holder of the Ericsson technique. It costs about Rs. 4,000 per insemination. Of the first 100 couples to come to her clinic, 96 wanted sons and only four wanted daughters. Two-thirds of her clients were from the business community.

Once the sperm has been separated by using one of the methods mentioned above, the woman has to undergo ultrasound to pinpoint her ovulation timing. After that she is artificially inseminated with the sex-selected sperm of husband or donor. This entire procedure may have to be repeated 3-4 times to ensure pregnancy. If the woman conceives there is still a 25 percent chance that she may have conceived a child of the 'wrong' (in most cases, female) sex. Therefore she would still have to undergo amniocentesis or Chorionic villous biopsy, and in the event of a 'mistake', an abortion or repeated abortions, at the cost of her health.

3. CHISBO-FA-001 Technique

It is a new imported gadget introduced in 1996 in some select south Delhi hospitals. In appearance like a hi-tech digital alarm clock, it is based on regulating the timing of intercourse with 'identifiable' points in the menstrual cycle. Fed with data pertaining to the first day of the cycle, it is said to indicate with 98 percent accuracy the chances of conceiving a boy or a girl on a given date. The CHISBO is based on the hypothesis that X- and Y-chromosome carrying sperm have a different lifespan and motility. If coitus occurs at the time of ovulation when the ovum is waiting for fertilization, the chances of conceiving a boy are said to be greater as the Y-chromosome carrying sperm would reach the ovum first. The use of marketing of such a gadget is not punishable under the Pre-Natal Diagnostic Techniques (Regulation and Prevention of Misuse) Act.

(b) Postconceptional Sex Detection

1. Amniocentesis

Amniocentesis was first advocated for diagnostic purpose in 1930. In 1951, Rosa and Fanaed described a method of foetal sex determination by amniotic fluid cytology. In 1965, the technique was used for antenatal diagnosis of hereditary diseases. In India, amniocentesis was first introduced in 1974 at the All India Institute of Medical Sciences in New Delhi to detect foetal abnormalities. But today amniocentesis has become synonymous with sex determination tests. That is to determine whether the unborn child is male or female, and if female, to abort it. Amniocentesis is very expensive in other countries and under strict government control but in India not only upper and middle classes but even lower class people can afford to avail it.

The human foetus lies in the uterus contained in the amniotic sac and surrounded by the amniotic fluid. Cells from the foetus are passed into the amniotic fluid. These are collected by a simple method of passing a needle through the abdominal wall of the pregnant woman. 15-20 ml. of amniotic fluid is taken out and examined to know of congenital defects and other diseases in the unborn child. Chromosomal analysis for sex determination involves checking for the presence of a stainable dot in the nucleus of the cells. The spot (known as the Barr body) is usually present in females and absent in males. Another test, using a dye called quinacrine, looks for what is called fluorescent bodies in the nucleus. The presence of these bodies indicates a male foetus. Though other methods are available to determine genetic diseases or abnormalities, amniocentesis is most widely used all over the world.

Sex determination is essential only in cases of genetic diseases which are sex-linked such as hemophilia and which cannot be diagnosed by any other means. This test is also routinely used for women after 40 years of age when they are more likely to produce deformed children. Amniocentesis is usually being done at 16th week of pregnancy for accurate determination of the sex; cell-culture for 3 weeks is required. At times, test has to be repeated. Chromosomal analysis including sex analysis without culturing the cells are subject to error in nearly 10- 20% of cases. In practice, the cells are generally not cultured.

2. Chorion Villous Biopsy

With this technique, one could diagnose hereditary diseases and congenital defects in an unborn foetus as early as seven weeks after conception. But, today, this technique is used largely to know the sex of an unborn child. It is performed in the first seven to eleven weeks of pregnancy under strict aseptic conditions. A plastic cannula is passed through cervix or through abdominal route up to the optimum site and a few chorionic cells are aspirated under ultrasound vision. These cells are cultured in a specific solution. Examination of these cultured cells that give information about the growing foetus reveals also its sex.

3. Ultrasonography

This is the most widely used method for sex determination these days. Ultrasonography is being used in obstetrics and gynecology for nearly three decades but its use for determining the sex of the foetus is only ten to fifteen years old. It is done at about fourteen to sixteen weeks of pregnancy. Since it is noninvasive, the test has gained immense popularity as prenatal sex determination technique. Such centers have been mushrooming even in small towns. In Haryana, even in small town and villages weekly mobile services are offered for the same purpose. Once known that the foetus is female; a mild-trimester abortion is carried out either by an expert doctor or by a dai in the remote areas.

But in spite of all the efforts done by the government and its machinery, female foeticide has become more rampant with the declining child sex ratio as its testimony. Arguments both supporting and opposing sex determination (SD) are being made (Macklin, 1995).

The leading arguments in support of SD are:

1. ***Through SD one can get rid of unwanted daughters and beget the preferred offspring.***

2. ***Women would be relieved of the burden of repeated pregnancies and producing children till a son is born.***

3. ***Parents would be relieved of economic burden in the form of dowry to girl.***

The major arguments opposing SD are:

1. ***The practice devalues the female sex.***

2. ***It reinforces current attitudes and practices that discriminate against girl children and women.***

3. ***It results in an imbalance in the sex ratio.***

Imbalance in sex ratio may lead to drastic consequences such as polyandry, forced prostitution, increase in crimes like rape, incest kidnapping etc. Experience from China and from Haryana (Gertrude, 2005) and Uttar Pradesh (The Tribune, 2005) reiterates the damages of sex ratio imbalance.

A Few Authentic Reports on Son Preference and Female Foeticide in India

Miller (1981) considers that sex-selection of offspring would at least reduce the number of unwanted and hence neglected (if not murdered) daughters, although no excess of boys, apparently, will change the incorrigible preference for them. She seems to lend tacit approval to the practice when she says 'such a method' if proven safe for users, would solve many problems'. The sufferings borne by unwanted daughters would end, as would the impaired health of mothers who bear more children than they otherwise would if the birth of sons were more assured. Her only problem seems to be that the sex ratio would become further skewed against females.

Dharma (1983) argues that sex selection at conception will reduce the supply of women, they will become more valuable, and female children will be better cared for and will live longer. We have here a good instrument for balancing the supply and demand for women, and for equating their price all over India (since caste, regional, religious and other barriers prevent the movement of women) so that in course of time one should expect dowries to fall in the North.

Jeffery et al. (1984) observe that while historically female infanticide was prevalent among the warrior castes such as the Rajputs and Jats, female foeticide is prevalent in all communities. Even today, differential rates of child mortality are noted for females in rural areas and differentials in sex ratio of the rural population in Uttar Pradesh, Punjab, Haryana, Rajasthan, Gujarat, in contrast to states in south and east India. Male bias in sex ratio is known to be more region-specific to a particular religion.

A study conducted by Kulkarni (1986), a gynecologist at the Foundation for Research in Community Health (FRCR) in Bombay, at the initiative of the state government of Maharashtra revealed that 64.3 percent of the 42 gynecologists interviewed were performing amniocentesis solely for sex determination purposes. These 42 doctors together performed on an average of 271 sex determination tests per month. Only in less than 10 percent of the cases was the test carried out for detection of genetic defects. Some said they had been performing the test for 10-12 years. The majority of the doctors said their clients came mainly from the middle class, a few from the upper class, and a very small number from the lower class. In the majority of the cases the women who came for the tests had two or three daughters; only about 10 percent of the women had one or more sons.

Kulkarni also opines that in developing countries like India, as the parents are encouraged to limit their family to two offsprings, they will have a right to quality in these two as far as can be assured. Obviously, by 'quality' what is meant here are male children.

Balasubramanian (1986) reports that Dr. D.N. Pai, an influential figure in the Indian family planning establishment, strongly advocated the use of sex determination tests within India's family planning programme. In 1974, at a conference in Stockholm, Dr. Pie described amniocentesis followed by abortion of the female foetus as a possible 'solution' to India's population growth.

According to Dharma (1988) one cannot cure social prejudice merely by legislation, especially in countries like India where the governmental machinery is weak and corruption rampant. Instead of bringing more unwanted girls into the world, surely it would be better to improve the lives and status of those who are born. It will choke off a powerful method of lowering the birth rate with out coercion.

Lingam (1989) suggests that although there are those who argue that the market forces of supply and demand will result in women acquiring a higher status once they are in short supply, research studies on societies with adverse female sex ratios have indicated the presence of customs like polyandry (which in reality means being used by more men), abduction and purchase of women. Also, adverse sex ratios are bound to increase the incidence of rape, prostitution and violence against women.

Patel (1989) argues that legislation banning sex-detection tests would definitely take away the respectability attached to this scientific advancement aggressively advocated by our doctors with crude, anti-women advertisements. According to her this preserve use of technology is encouraged and boosted by money-minded practitioners who are out to make Indian women male producing machines. Many parishioners have invested large sums of money in equipment, particularly in ultrasound machines, and they see this as a quick way to recover this investment.

Sen (1990) by using the term 'missing women' drew attention to the declining ratio of women to men in large parts of Asia and Africa. He attributed this to a combination of factors that included patriarchy, male preference and female illiteracy.

Thaneja (1991) undertook a survey in the city of Delhi to elicit the opinions of males and females regarding the social and moral aspects of female foeticide which showed that a significantly higher percentage of the female respondents expressed a positive opinion about female foeticide, both overall and aspect-wise, as compared to male respondents, among whom none held a positive opinion.

Kimbrell (1993) reports that, in 1991, about 100, 00 female foetuses were aborted after sex determination test. A memorandum submitted to the Prime Minister by the Women's Cultural Association of Ahmedabad in the state of Gujarat reports that out of 35,000 sex determination tests conducted, about 18,000 were followed by an abortion. Some of the aborted foetuses are sold and even exported to Europe for research and cell transplants.

Kusum (1993) shares her fears regarding the imbalance between the sexes that may result from sex selective abortions. According to her it may end up in polyandry and increase in crimes like rape, incest and kidnapping. She also mentions the fear that the reproductive burden on women will increase because the same burden of bringing forth progeny will then have to be shared by fewer women.

According to a report by Kaul (1993), three baby girls are killed every month in the capital city of Delhi. These deaths are mainly confined to the shanty towns and resettlements colonies of East and West Delhi inhabited mainly by the lower working class. Acute poverty, the lack of knowledge about abortion facilities, or a lack of facilities itself and gender bias appear to be the main reasons for this.

Glover (1994) predicts the consequences of an imbalance in sex ratio. Glover speculates that if two thirds of a generation were male, a real problem could result. Men would feel that they are at a substantial disadvantage since many of them would be deprived of a partner. This in turn, could result in a growth in prostitution and pressures towards polyandry. Glover rejects the argument of a positive consequence of imbalanced sex ratio whereby value of women in society would increase on the grounds that it depends on an excessively economic view of relationships and of why people are valued. Even though scarcity drives up the value of any commodity, people are not commodities and so the benefit to women from the imbalance is at least highly speculative.

Macklin (1995) argues that while sex determination (SD) is not a desirable practice, prohibiting it by law is likely to do more harm than good. No rights are violated when SD is allowed by law and that legal prohibition of SD will infringe upon the reproductive rights of women.

Sudha and Rajan (1996) reports that exogamous marriage makes women vulnerable by separating them from their natal families and at the same time placing them amongst marital families who are virtual strangers. In such situations of extreme vulnerability one of the ways to gain acceptance and prove themselves as 'good' daughters in-law is to give birth to sons.

George (1997) and others have pointed to the fact that a small family norm is not necessarily accompanied by a preference for a fewer number of sons. Son-preference continues to be a significant determinant in family building strategies.

The National Family Health Survey (NFHS-II, 1998-99) collected information on the role that son preference plays in determining family planning practices. At the all-India level 83 percent of every married woman in the age group 15-49 with two sons and 76 percent with one son said they did not want any more children. On the other hand significantly fewer women, 47 percent, with two daughters said they did not want more children.

According to Singh (1998) women themselves enthusiastically go for the prenatal sex determination tests and female foeticide of their free will. It is said to be a question of women's own choice. But these women are conditioned in such socio-cultural environment that they try to prove their social worth and value by producing a male child.

George (2000) opines that the reasons for the female foeticide might be the introduction and proliferation of parental diagnostic tests, sex determination clinics and cheaper ultrasound machines that help determine the sex of child before it is born. Dramatic reduction of birth rates in most of India's states has contributed to intensification of son-preference in the existing patriarchal society.

Gupta (2000) reports that Dr. Bhandari of the New Bhandari Hospital in Amritsar announced his unique savings scheme in a handbill with tempting slogan: 'Spend Rs. 500 now and save Rs. 500,000 later' – meaning, spend a paltry sum now on the test and, by comparison, save a huge amount later which you may have to spend on the dowry of a daughter. This was a call for sex selective abortion without explicitly saying so. Gupta further considers the phenomenon of female infanticide and foeticide needs to be analyzed in the context of economic marginalization as a result of modernization process, illiteracy, as well as deep-rooted traditions and customs, the low/negative value attached to women in Indian society, as reasons for boy preference.

Sen (2001) identifies seven types of gender inequalities existing in most parts of the world. Natality inequality being one among them has become common with the availability of modern techniques to determine the gender of the foetus whereby the female foetus is selectively aborted. This high-tech sexism is particularly prevalent in East Asia, in China and South Korea in particular, in Singapore and Taiwan and is beginning to emerge as a statistically significant phenomenon in India and South Asia.

According to Mallik (2002), during the past two decades the average family size has been declining. This has been a result of voluntary acceptance by couples of smaller families, in response to a number of economic and social changes and partly due to the government's efforts to hasten the transition through the family planning program. Mallik further suggests that the use of coercive measures in implementing population policies particularly undue emphasis on the use of terminal methods can easily lead to an intensifying trend towards sex determination and sex selective abortion.

Patel (2002) expresses her concern over the adverse juvenile sex ratio in Kerala. According to her threat of desertion, divorce and ill treatment force women to opt for sex determination and abortion. The masculinisation of the younger generation as per Patel could only be attributed to selective abortion of female foetus after the use of ultra sound scanning techniques. She opposes the argument that the dearth of girls in the long run would enhance the social value of daughters. This is not applicable to a patriarchal society like that of India where sexuality and fertility of women are controlled by men.

According to Arnold et al. (2003) son preference and abortion can be linked in two distinct ways. First through the specific use of SD and SSA to identify and eliminate female foetuses and the second is abortion. These decisions purportedly appear to be for family planning but the sex of living children constitutes an important basis for the decision.

Rutherford and Roy (2003) use NFHS- II data to point out that the trend of sex preference appears to be strongest in families that already have two children. This they attribute to the fact that the current total fertility rate (TFR) for India is about three and a large proportion of women wish to stop childbearing after having three children. A strong sex preference, mainly for sons, clearly determines the third birth order.

According to Agnivesh et al. (2005), female foeticide which has been presumed to be most prevalent among the poor and illiterate because of spiraling dowry demands and other traditional prejudices are today most frequent among the rich and highly educated. They report a study that maps the increased frequency of female foeticide with rising levels of education, lowest among women with a fifth grade education and highest among women with university degrees. Also assumed to be prevalent among Hindus because of their custom requiring male progeny to perform cremation rites, female foeticide is found today to be equally rampant among Sikhs, Muslims and Christians. It is pointed out that ending female foeticide alone will not bring about desirable results but all forms of gender injustice must be stopped.

Gertrude (2005) highlighted the grave situation created by sex selective technology in Haryana. Quoting the 2001 Census Report and the low sex ratio in Haryana, she illustrated the consequences of adverse sex ratio. Young men in Haryana are finding it difficult to obtain brides and have resorted to buying brides from far away states of Assam and Bengal. She made an observation that these brides after begetting a son were left to fend for themselves. She also mentioned a practice where a woman is married by a man and bedded by his brothers too.

The Hindu (2005) reports the findings of the study conducted by the Centre for Social Research in Delhi that preference for a male child is higher among the educated and rich sections of the society. Accordingly the rich and educated class has greater access to ultrasound clinics where sex determination tests of the foetus are done. Poor implementation of the PNDT act is projected as a major reason for the declining sex ratio. The report also says that the Birth Registration Data made available by the Municipal Corporation of Delhi showed that the sex ratio at birth in Delhi between January and June 2004 indicated that only 819 girls were born for every 1000 boys. The Centre for Social Research has sought transparency in the government's actions for civil society to be vigilant and to contribute to official efforts.

Sulaja (2005) analysed the link between gender preference and contraceptive acceptance by women in four southern states of India namely, Andhra Pradesh, Karnataka, Kerala and Tamil Nadu. According to the NFHS-II data, it has been observed that the number of sons in the family is the sole deciding factor in the acceptance of contraception by women in all the four states. The findings further reveal that the average number of sons was more than daughters in all the states under study. Son preference was comparatively low in Kerala as compared to Andhra Pradesh and the chance of accepting permanent methods of contraception was more when the family had more number of sons or at least one son.

According to Vyas (2005) the extermination of girls through female foeticide would lead to major imbalances that can destroy the social and human fabric of society. She reports a case of a family in remote Uttar Pradesh where one girl was married to four boys due to scarcity of girls. She stresses the need to review the Abortion Act. She also points out the trauma and suffering the woman undergoes while subjecting herself to sex selective abortion.

Aravamudan (2007) through her book on 'Disappearing Daughters: The Tragedy of Female Foeticide' presents an in depth account of the growing practice of female foeticide in India. According to her though India has a history of skewed female sex ratio, what the country is witnessing today is the systematic extermination of the female child, with the ultrasound machine serving as an instrument of murder. The prosperous urban areas play role models to impoverished rural India and this shared value, an all-consuming preference for sons, spans the urban rural divide and cuts across shameful disparities in consumption patterns and nutrition levels and translates into girl baby murder. The author cautions that if the macabre practice continues, it would spell doom for both sons and daughters and will have a disastrous impact on the future generations.

Inference drawn from the reviewed reports

Son preference is a discriminatory practice prevailing in almost all states of the country. The declining trend in child sex ratio through out the country and its various states has been attributed to strong son preference and subsequent female foeticide by several investigators. The reports of nation-wide surveys in this regard have been substantiated by researches done in the area. This obsession for sons leads to the widespread use of the sex determination techniques and elimination of the female foetus.

The availability of NRTs in the emerging multi specialty hospitals and the mushrooming ultrasound scanning centers in the private sector have boosted up the trend for sex selective abortions. Even though female foeticide emerged in the urban belt, it has moved on to the rural areas also cutting across class and caste.

Several surveys and research studies have proved that son preference and subsequent sex selective abortions are more prevalent among the rich and educated classes. It is also shown that son preference increases with decreasing family size. All these findings in the backdrop of a declining child sex ratio point to the existence of son preference and probability of female foeticide in the Kerala society where the people are highly educated and strictly adhering to small family norms.

The review of the study reveals that the overall sex ratio of Kerala is highlighted by all investigators. The declining child sex ratio of the state has not gained much attention. Only very few studies have been done on the issue in Kerala. The fairly good overall sex ratio of Kerala is masking the hidden grave situation.

A thorough analysis of the extent of son preference in the Kerala society would serve to understand the linkage if any between the discriminatory practice and the declining child sex ratio. The analysis of reasons attributed to son preference would help in designing policies and programmes at various levels to nip the evil in the bud. Several authors have expressed their fears regarding the far reaching consequences of sex ratio imbalance.

4

Design of the Study

The attempt to trace the existence and extent of son preference in Kerala society was taken up as a survey. The reasons for the anomaly with regard to the favourable sex ratio of the total population and the unfavorable child sex ratio were explored. An analysis of the reasons attributed to son preference in the society by various categories of people is also undertaken.

The specific concept of 'missing women' originally coined by Nobel Laureate Amartya Sen connotes 'that population of females who are expected to be present as per demographic norms but at the same time are not present due to specific reasons at a specific point of time'. The concept was devised to give an idea of the enormity of the phenomena of women's adversity in mortality by focusing on the women who are simply not there due to unusually high mortality compared with male mortality rates. There exists a quantitative difference between (1) the actual number of women in several of the South Asian countries, and (2) the number one could expect to see if the gender pattern of mortality were similar in these countries as in other regions of the world that do not have a significant bias against women in terms of health care and other attributes relevant for survival. But the state of Kerala in India provides a sharp contrast with many other parts of the country in having little or no gender bias in mortality leading to a fair female-male ratio of 1.06 according to the 2001 Census. But where gone are the 79,760 girls (Kerala Sastra Sahithya Parishad, 2006) in the age group of 0-6 years who should have been present in the Kerala population as per demographic norms (Census, 2001). The concept of "missing girls" by Patel (2002) to represent this population is used in the present study. As pointed out by several researchers strong son preference leading to sex selective abortions or female foeticide which is a common discriminatory practice proved to exist in educated and prosperous states of the country is hypothesized to be the reason behind the missing girls phenomenon of Kerala state also. The increasing number of super specialty hospitals in the private sector and the mushrooming ultra sound scanning centers support the assumption of female foeticide to be responsible for unfavorable child sex ratio in the state.

Sample for the Study

In the present study the population is the reproductively active men and women in the age group of 20-40 years. This is done in order to study the impact of the choices and attitudes of the particular group on the child sex ratio. Even though the unfavorable child sex ratio is visible since 1985 it has become so remarkable during the last six or seven years. Hence it was decided to include only the reproductively active age group in the present investigation, which as per Kerala's cultural practices vary from 20-40 years. The sample consisting of 450 individuals was selected using stratified random sampling method. Gender, locale, religion, education and income levels were used as the classificatory variables for identifying the various sub samples.

(a) Factors considered in the selection of the sample

Several studies have reported that the number of missing girls is more among the urban people than their counterparts in the rural settings (Aravamudan, 2007). The easy availability of advanced reproductive technologies in the multi specialty hospitals in urban areas might be a factor responsible for elimination of girl child through sex selection techniques. Hence in the present study locale was also taken as a classificatory variable to study the regional influence on son preference and female foeticide. The sample for the present study consists of 230 respondents from the urban area and 220 respondents from the rural area.

According to the First Report on Religion Data (2001), there is considerable difference in child sex ratios among various religious communities, as given in Table 4.

TABLE 4
Sex Ratio among various Religious Communities

Religious Communities	*Child Sex Ratio*	*Overall Sex Ratio*
Hindus	925	931
Muslims	950	936
Jains	870	940
Sikhs	786	836
Christians	964	1009
Buddhists	942	953
Others	976	992
All	927	933

Table 4 shows that the child sex ratio and overall sex ratio vary considerably with the religious communities. There are 931 Hindu women for every 1000 Hindu men, which is less than the National average of 933 women for every 1000 men.

The figure among Muslim community is 936 per 1000. Christians have the highest sex ratio of 1009 females per 1000 males and Sikhs record the lowest overall sex ratio of 839 per 1000. With regard to child sex ratio, it was the worst among Sikhs, then Jains, followed by the Hindus and Buddhists while that of Muslims and Christians was better.

Taking the above facts into consideration it was decided to include an equal number of subjects from the three major religious communities of Kerala, viz, Hindus, Christians and Muslims in the sample for study. The sample thus consists of 150 Hindus, 150 Christians and 150 Muslims. The religion – wise split-up of the sample is given in Table 5.

TABLE 5
Religion-wise Split up of the Sample

Sample	*Christian*	*Hindu*	*Muslim*	*Total*
Men	75	75	75	225
Women	75	75	75	225
Total	150	150	150	450

Preference for a male child seems to be higher among the educated and rich sections of the society (The Hindu, 2005). As per the study conducted by the Centre for Social Research, Delhi, in the prosperous and educated south Delhi Zone, the girl-boy sex ratio below five years has declined to 762 girls born for every 1000 boys. It is suggested that the rich and educated classes have greater access to ultrasound clinics where sex determination tests of the foetus are done surreptitiously. The Census Report (2001) itself reveals that female foeticide is prevalent mostly among the prosperous states of Punjab, Haryana, Rajasthan and Gujarat. Considering the effect of education and income levels on attitudes and out-looks and the evidences obtained from the Census details (2001), it was decided to include education and income levels also for classifying the total sample into sub groups.

(b) Classification technique for identifying the sub-samples

(i) Classification Based on Education Levels

The total sample was divided into three sub groups viz. High-, Average- and Low Education groups based on the following criteria:

Up to 10th standard	:	Low Education group
Up to Degree	:	Average Education group
Postgraduate / Professional	:	High Education group

The number of subjects coming under the High-, Average and Low Education groups were 162, 180 and 108 respectively.

(ii) Classification Based on Income Levels

The income levels of the sample showed much variation. The total sample was divided into three sub groups viz. High-, Average- and Low Income groups based on their monthly income as per the following criteria:

Up to Rs. 5,000	:	Low Income group
Rs. 5001 – Rs. 15,000	:	Average Income group
Above Rs. 15,000	:	High Income group

TABLE 6

Distribution of the Final Sample Based on Education and Income Levels

Variable	*High*	*Average*	*Low*	*Total*
Education	162	180	108	450
Income	132	168	150	450

The number of subjects coming under the High- Average – and Low- Income groups were 132, 168 and 150 respectively.

Split up of the final sample based on education and income levels is given in Table 6.

(c) Procedure of Selecting the Sample

Parents of first standard students belonging to 6 schools each of the two districts viz. Ernakulam and Malappuram consisting of an equal number of men and women participated in the study. Gender, locale, religion, education and income levels were used as the classificatory variables for identifying the various sub samples. Since the sample was selected giving due weightage to the various strata involved, it could well be conceived as a representative group of the society with different religions, education and income levels.

The Tool Used

A Son Preference Inventory was used by the investigator for the collection of data. Common beliefs in favour of boy child and against the girl child were included in the inventory. The first part of the inventory assesses the demographic details of the respondents such as gender, locale, religion, education, and income levels. The second part collects data on respondent's response towards the existence of son preference and attitude towards female foeticide. The response to the question 'Do you think that son preference exists in the Kerala society' is to be marked with a tick mark in the appropriate box provided against 'Yes' or 'No' responses. Three responses were given to assess the general attitude towards female foeticide viz. 'It is to be condemned', 'It may be permitted if the situation demands' and 'There is nothing wrong with it'. Here also the respondent is to put a tick mark in the appropriate box given against the three responses.

The third part of the inventory contains ten statements, which are the reasons generally, conceived as responsible for son preference in the country. In India sons enjoy a great deal of social prestige. Only men can perform the traditional ancestor cult. Since girls marry into another family, only sons can guarantee for the care of the parents in old age. The family name is passed down through sons in the country. In societies where families have to pay a dowry when their daughters marry, the practice of discrimination against daughters is far more widespread. In the last two decades fuelled by a consumer boom among the new Indian middle class, dowry has spread like an epidemic to communities that never practiced it before. Another belief leading to son preference is that males are smarter and stronger than females and a female experiences much insecurity in the society. Girl children in poor families are being neglected in favour of their male siblings and are often denied adequate food and medical treatment. Hence the belief that a female's life is tragic makes parents crave for a male child. In Kerala society the traditional preference for sons has been reinforced by its lowest fertility rates and observance of small family norms.

The inventory requires the respondents to rank these statements in the order of 1 to 10 with the most prominent reason they find to be ranked as '1' and the least plausible reason assigned a rank of '10'.

A copy of the Son Preference Inventory (SPI) is given as Appendix III.

Procedure of Data Collection and Consolidation of Data

After fixing up the sample, the investigator contacted the Heads of the schools concerned for obtaining permission for administration of the tool. A time schedule was also fixed for the administration of tools well in advance.

Care was taken to get a representative sample that included parents belonging to the three major religious sectors –Hindu, Christian and Muslim belonging to different socio-economic strata. In the schools with the help of the Principals, Mother PTAs were called upon. After establishing rapport with the respondents the significance of the study was explained to them. The procedure for assigning ranks to the statements was demonstrated. One half of the mothers were entrusted with the responsibility of getting the inventories filled up by their husbands at home. The completed son preference inventories were collected from the schools the very next day.

The percentage of responses that ranked the first statement as No.1 reason was calculated. Similarly the percentage of ranking for all the ten statements was calculated. The consolidation was done by keeping in view the important sub samples to be obtained viz, the gender, locale and religious groups. Separate entries were also made for respondents belonging to the three major education and income levels viz., High, Average and Low.

Statistical Techniques Used

Percentage analysis was used to assess the extent of son preference in the total sample and the sub samples formed on the basis of the classificatory variables. In order to study the effect of the classificatory variables viz, gender, locale, religion, education and income levels on the attitude towards son preference and the nature of reasons attributed to son preference, chi-square test of independence of attributes was also employed.

5

Behind the Women Development Indicators

A profile of Kerala state, its demographic characteristics, the socio – economic prospects of the region and an account of the status of women as determined by various women development indices along with the truth hidden behind the indicators are detailed in this chapter. The rationale for selecting the two districts, viz. Ernakulam and Malappuram for conducting the present study is also given in detail.

Kerala occupying the south -western tip of Indian subcontinent has a total area of 38, 863 sq.km with a population of 318.38 lakhs (2001 census), which constitutes 3.34% of total population of India. It has 14 districts. The sex ratio is 1058 women for 1000 men, Infant Mortality Rate is 14, and Birth Rate is 18 and Death Rate 6.4. The Literacy rate is 90.92%. There are a total of 12318 schools in the state and seven Higher Education Universities.

Geographically, Kerala is divided into three major tourist regions such as Northern region; Central region and Western region. The two districts of Ernakulam and Malappuram selected for the present study belong to the Central and Northern regions respectively. The special features of the state can be summarized as follows:

Special Features:

- First literate state of India.
- First state to implement land reform bills and education reform bills.
- Lower birth rate.
- Least infant mortality.
- State with maximum life expectancy.
- The only state with the facilities of hospitals in every village.
- Excellent communication infrastructure.
- One among the states where air, water and road are used as the media for transportation.

Status of Women in Kerala

Conventional indicators like sex ratio, literacy, maternal mortality, morbidity, life expectancy etc. show that Kerala has achieved remarkably well but when each indicator is taken up for serious scrutiny, there are several contradictions. Similarly unconventional indicators like political participation, work participation rate, violence against women etc. also show that the status of women in Kerala is not as rosy as it is portrayed.

Kerala has been considered to be unique in many aspects as compared to the rest of India. In spite of having a poor economy, lower per capita income and unemployment, the state of Kerala has been known to achieve a quality of life, which is higher than all the other states in India and as equal to that of some developed countries. Kerala is often quoted for its high achievements in the field of health and family welfare at a low cost. This unique phenomenon of socio-economic development has also been very widely referred to as the 'Kerala Model of Development' (Zachariah, 1998). Kerala ranks the highest among the Indian states in HDI with a value of 62.8 followed by Maharashtra with an HDI of 55.49. A comparison of the conventional indicators of Kerala with that of India is given in Table 7.

TABLE 7
Conventional Indicators – Kerala and India

Indicators	*Kerala*	*India*
Sex Ratio (for 1000 males)	1058	927
Literacy (%)	88 (women) 94 (men)	54 (women) 74 (men)
Life expectancy of women	73.1 (67.1 for men)	65.43
Maternal mortality per (1000 live births)	1.3	5.7
Child death rate/1000	14.0	73.0
Birth rate/1000	16.0	27.2
Work participation rate (%)	15.8	22.3
Age at marriage	22	18

Source: Census 2001; Economic Review, Government of Kerala 2002 & 2003; NFHS-II 1998-99.

In general, Kerala is said to achieve a high physical quality of life in terms of literacy, life expectancy and infant mortality, at low per capita income. However, these developmental indicators do not go hand in hand with its progress in the material production sectors. There continues to be economic stagnation, increasing unemployment and a fall in the per capita income.

The gender development indicators show a higher status of women in the state. Kerala tops the list in terms of the reproductive health index of 84.61 (Srinivasan et al., 1997). The National Family Health Survey II (1998-1999) found that 93% of the births in Kerala took place with medical facilities.

The state is favorably placed when it comes to sex ratio with 1058 females for 1000 males (2001 census). But, when it comes to sex ratio of children in the 0-6 age group, there is an unfavorable trend (963:1000). There are debates about whether Kerala is gradually inclining towards the national scenario where there is increased male bias or whether this is a natural biological phenomenon, which evens out when we look at sex ratio from age 10 onwards.

Life expectancy of women in Kerala is 73 years, which is greater than that of men at 67 in Kerala. About 11% of the population is in the 60+ categories and there are 1120 females to 1000 men in this category. Increasing lifespan without adequate resources has led to increasing dependency, loneliness and insecurity among old women.

With respect to education, literacy rates are the highest in the country with 88% literacy for women but there are sex differences with a male literacy at 94%. Primary education is satisfactory but with reference to women's technical, vocational and professional education, Kerala is far behind other states. Currently women far exceed men in graduate and postgraduate education in the arts and science courses. But women forms less than one-third of the students enrolled in engineering colleges in recent years (GOK, 2001). Data on trade-wise intake for the year 2000-2001 reveals a preponderance of women in stenography, dressmaking, cutting and tailoring, secretarial practice and data preparation. Women have limited entry into masculine specializations but dominate those already identified with them. People are more aware of their needs and rights, conscious of their status and are generally demanding the services.

Work participation rate of women is lower than the national average. Women have not entered into non-stereotypical professions in a large way. Even marketing by women is not yet accepted. Women rarely have control over the income they earn. Women's income is used for children's education, health and for repaying debts whereas men's income is mostly used for building assets in their own name. Even if it is in joint name, authority is wielded by men. Money received as dowry also increases assets for men.

In relation to work within the family, patriarchal norms reign. Men hardly help in the domestic chores. There is no recognition for the work that women do within the family. High workload and household responsibility for women keep them away from public and social life. To manage all the household responsibilities such as shopping, cooking, cleaning, washing, taking care of the children, attending PTA meetings of school going children, taking the kids to the doctors, looking after the aged are all responsibilities of women.

Kerala is well known as a state with high degree of male migration. This leaves many families where women have to be head of the households. Hence, the number of female-headed households is high in the state.

Women owning assets and having control over them also is low in a state where matriliny is supposed to have prevailed in some community. As per the Economic Review published by the Kerala State Planning Board in 2001, women hold only 23.18% of the operational holdings in the state. Women own only 17.16% percentage of the total area under operational holdings.

Kerala is far ahead of other states of the country with regard to its health status. Maternal mortality and infant mortality rates are low. Yet, the population control achieved through remarkable family planning methods emphasized the control of female fertility as its sole means. Maternal mortality per 1000 live births is 1.3 and infant mortality rate per 1000 is 14% and birth rate is 16% and the age of marriage is 22 years (Census 2001, Economic Review, Government of Kerala 2002 & 2003 and NFHS II 1998-99).

Kerala has achieved all the major health indicators targeted for "Health For All by 2000 AD". It would be worthwhile to look at this juncture beyond 2000 AD in the context of the global discussion of 'Zero Population Growth'. Kerala may attain birth rate of about 10 per thousand in another 20 to 25 years. The death rate has almost stabilized around 6 per thousand. The economic and social development factors leading to women's emancipation and the tendency to avoid child birth as far as possible and limitation to one child will not be a distant dream in the demographic profile of Kerala. Sterilization of women is the commonly practiced method playing a severe toll on women's reproductive, physical and mental health. Over-commercialization and privatization of health services has affected women's health. Women hardly have any control over their own body, and sexuality. Men have never owned up sexual responsibility.

With respect to marital status and type of family, several women are divorced, deserted and separated. With respect to marriage, women hardly have any choice in relation to whom or where or when she should be married. This has led to unhealthy events like Mali, Haryana and Mysore kalyanam (Kalyanam means marriage in Malayalam) which are specific types of interstate marriages where Keralite girls are sent into wedlock with natives and residents of those regions just for the sake of getting legally married and having children legally. Women in interstate marriages will have to face serious problems like the unfamiliar language, culture, poor life situations, economic dependence, domestic violence etc. Even after experiencing these painful life situations, the married girls never get any security from their husbands or in laws. Most of them are treated brutally with violence, negligence, poverty, starvation and finally desertion. A few numbers of girls are living with their husbands, fighting a life at the strange place with strange language and strange customs. Most of them are deserted, but not legally divorced and get nothing for their survival. Because of the over importance of marriage and the stereo typical roles assigned to women, the human rights violations behind the closed doors are neglected socially and politically.

Dowry is fast replacing property rights and the rate has escalated. The dowry system has become a strong custom in all castes, classes and communities within the past two - three decades. Dowry is under the control of men and is usually spent after marriage to fulfill marriage expenditure. The institution of marriage mainly rests on the transaction of money and goods. This trading is inversely related to education, class and caste. The 'status study of women in Kerala' by Sakhi Women's Resource Centre (2006) reveals that with increase in education, dowry is also escalating. The study of Mahila Samakhya Society (2008-09) on 'status of women in Nilambur grama panchayath of Malappuram district' highlights the issue of dowry as a major cause for interstate marriages (Mysore kalyanam) and the subsequent desertion of women by their husbands. When compared to the dowry rates in near by places, it is very low in Mysore marriages. Parents would go to any length to get their daughter married and keep her married at all costs rather than face the stigma of having an unmarried or divorced daughter at home.

Decision-making is an important determinant of the status of women. The NFHS II 1998-99 survey among women in Kerala related to autonomy of the women has questioned the claims of the so-called "high status" of Kerala women. The survey found that more than 50% of the women in Kerala needed permission to go to the market or visit friends or relatives (UNDP, 2001). Very few women have any say even with respect to the purchase of food, clothes, gold or costly equipment. Even in families when women are the major income earners, decision-making rests with men. The facts that abortion is still now used as a method of contraception by women and Kerala ranks second among states with highest incidence of abortions (NFHS II) show the lack of decision making power of Keralite women over their body and sexuality. The results of the study conducted by Kuruvilla and Aanand (2009) on 180 married women from Malappuram district of Kerala are also in agreement with that of the NFHS II survey findings. Nearly fifty percent of the respondents were found not to have any kind of decision making power. Only 33 percent were having power in financial matters, 37 percent in household affairs and 50 percent in children's affairs. 74 percent of the sample including highly employed ones needed the permission of their husbands to visit relatives. More than 50 percent of the total respondents do not have any power over dowry and other gifts they got from the relatives at the time of marriage. Though 29 percent have property in their names, only half of them do have any control over their assets.

In the recent years, there has been an increase in the cases of depression found among the women in the state. Keralite women are the highest consumers of tranquilisers in the country. The Indian Psychological Association makes repeated reports about the low mental health profiles of women in Kerala. There have been increasing cases of suicide and unnatural deaths. Most of this is associated with escalating rates of dowry, consumerism, high indebtedness, pawning of property and increasing rate of domestic violence. But this increasing trend of unnatural deaths has not led to the questioning of the high status of women projected by the state.

Women are victims of all forms of violence viz. mental, physical, economic, and sexual violence especially within their homes. As per the studies that have been conducted in Kerala on violence against women, they are victimized within home mostly by their husbands. A study conducted by ICRW (2002) on domestic violence in Kerala found that as high as 62.3% and 61.61% of the women in Kerala are subjected to physical torture and mental harassment as compared to 37% and 35.5% at the national level. The same study found that Thiruvananthapuram, the capital of Kerala ranked first among the five cities in India for the prevalence of domestic violence against women. The UNFPA commissioned study in Kerala (2005) carried out by the Sakhi Resource Centre for Women for the Department of Health, Government of Kerala reports 40% violence against women, with an average of 2 women patients coming to the

Out Patients Department (OPD) with injuries due to violence. There are increasing reports of dowry related violence, rape and other atrocities against women in Kerala (Women's Commission, 1999). This has been substantiated by other studies also. Belief in the propagation of patriarchal values and reinforcing stereotypes lead to violence. Power relations determine the family structure and dynamics. Mobility is severely affected due to eve teasing and molestation.

Women's political participation is abysmally low with women's membership in political parties and trade unions almost negligible. Women are merely used to enhance numbers in processions and strikes. Information in relation to services is almost nil. Political participation is yet another determinant of the status of women but in Kerala which is so politicized, out of 144 seats in the State Assembly, the number of women has never been more than 13 i.e. 10%. Women's representation is also low in the various decision-making bodies of the political parties and trade unions.

Profile of the Districts Selected for Study

Ernakulam

It is the most important city in Kerala. It is the second most important city on the Western coast of India. Ernakulam can be regarded as the commercial and industrial capital of Kerala. The demographic details are as follows:

Area	:	87.341 sq.km.
Population	:	2589038
Religion	:	Hindus account for the largest community followed by Christians and Muslims. There is also a small population of Jains, Jews and Sikhs.

Ernakulam, served by an international airport, fine communication facilities, excellent accommodation, modern amenities and a lot of attractive tourist places gives a breathtaking experience for its visitors and settlers. The district took its form on **1st April 1958**, by carving out the areas of erstwhile Travancore, Kochi & Malabar kingdoms. The word Ernakulam was derived from a Tamil word '*Erayanarkulam*' which means 'Lord Shiva's abode'.

Ernakulam is considered as the elite district of the elite state, which is mainly an industrial area and business centre with high standards of living. The good number of showrooms and offices of international business groups and firms offer large employment opportunities to the growing population. People have easy access to all modern amenities comparable to international standards and excellent health facilities with a large number of super specialty hospitals and diagnostic centers in the private sector.

Malappuram

It is the land of great poets and writers, political and religions leaders. It has a unique social and cultural heritage. Malappuram district was formed in June 1969 amalgamating the distant and backward areas of the erstwhile Kozhikode, Perintalmanna and Ponnani taluks of Palakkad. The Nilgiris (Blue Mountains) of Tamil Nadu in the east and the Arabian sea in the west, provide natural boundaries. In the north, it is bounded by Kozhikode and Waynad Districts and in the south, by Palakkad and Thrissur districts.

The district has carved a place of its own in the history of Kerala. The Kings of Valluvanad, the Zamorins, the kings of Perumpadappu Swarupam and the Kings of Vettathunadu, were the early rulers. Portuguese, Mysore Sultans and the Britishers, had their sway over this place, partly or wholly. But the unique social and cultural heritage is preserved. The demographic details are as follows:

Area	:	3550 sq.km.
Population	:	3, 096, 00

TABLE 8

Rural -Urban Distribution of Population in Kerala, Ernakulam and Malappuram Districts, 2001

State / District		*Population*			*0-6 Population*		
		P	*M*	*F*	*P*	*M*	*F*
	Total	31841374	15468614	16372760	3793146	1935027	1858119
Kerala	Rural	23574449	11451282	12123167	2857686	1457233	1400453
	Urban	8266925	4017332	4249593	935460	477794	457666
	Total	3105798	1538397	1567401	338924	173413	165511
Ernakulam	Rural	1628713	808609	820104	178029	91052	86977
	Urban	1477085	729788	747297	160895	82361	78534
	Total	3625471	1754576	1870895	281449	270076	2745398
Malappuram	Rural	3269301	1581794	1687507	254378	244375	2465937
	Urban	356170	172782	183388	27071	25701	279461

Source : Directorate of Census Operations Kerala 2001.

Religion : Muslims account for the largest community followed by Hindus and Christians.

The migration of men to gulf countries is especially pronounced in the area. Though the foreign remittances made by the gulf migrants have served a lot to boost the economy of the area, its impact on the social life, particularly that of the women left behind in the house has not always been very positive. The mean age at marriage in Malappuram is still very low when compared to the state average and the practice of teenage marriage of girls continues.

Malappuram is the least developed district of the state with relatively high rate of population growth, low public health status, low levels of education, lowest mean age of marriage and very low industrial and agricultural growth. Unlike Ernakulam where the majority follows small family norms, in Malappuram people show a reluctance to adopt family planning methods. Practices like polygamy, dowry, men's right to divorce at will, early marriage and adolescent childbirths are also a common feature of Malappuram. The female work participation rate of Ernakulam is 17.18% whereas it is 6.63% in Malappuram.

The rural – urban distribution of population in Kerala and the districts of Ernakulam and Malappuram are given in Table 8.

The child sex ratio of the two districts during the 1991 and 2001 Census are given in Table 9.

The gender gap in child sex ratio in favour of male child does not vary much with regard to Ernakulam during 1991 and 2001. But in the case of Malappuram this gender gap against girl child has doubled over the ten years period as evident from Figure 2.

TABLE 9
0-6 years Population of Ernakulam and Malappuram Districts during 1991 and 2001

District	*1991*		*2001*	
	Male	*Female*	*Male*	*Female*
Ernakulam	167866	159192	173413	165511
Gender gap in child ratio	8674		7902	
Malappuram	268482	262774	281449	270076
Gender gap in child ratio	5708		11373	

Source: Directorate of Census Operations, Kerala 2001.

The study was intended to assess whether son preference exists in the two districts of Ernakulam and Malappuram and if so what all reasons are attributed to this unfair practice. The attitude of people belonging to the two districts towards female foeticide was also studied. Since the two districts vary much with regard to their socio –economic and cultural aspects, a qualitative comparison between the extent of son preference and attitude towards female foeticide was also attempted.

Conclusion

An analysis of the demographic profiles of the two districts of Ernakulam and Malappuram reveals that the commercial capital, Ernakulam is highly advanced when compared to Malappuram. But the foreign remittances due to migration of men has resulted in bringing about certain socio-economic changes in Malappuram district also. But how far such changes have affected the outlooks and attitudes of men and women is a question yet to be researched. The two districts have contradictory socio cultural milieu as far as their demographic profiles are concerned. Ernakulam with its rich floating population has a mixed culture whereas Malappuram has comparatively a stagnant culture with mass migration of men

FIGURE 2

Gender Gap in Sex Ratio of Ernakulam and Malappuram

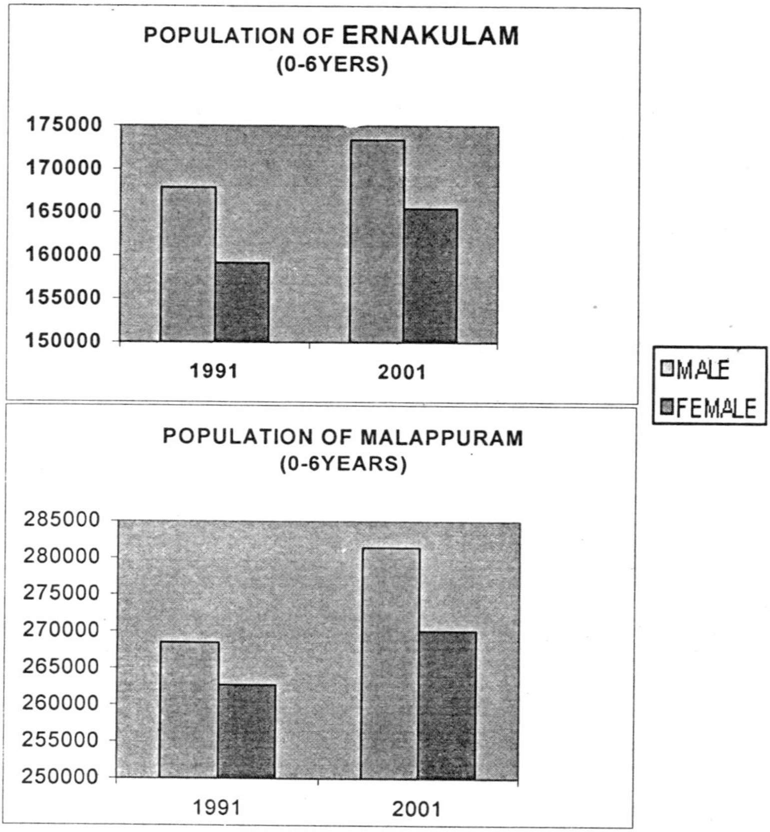

to gulf countries. People in Ernakulam adhere more to small family norms necessitated by their costly urban life whereas in Malappuram such a practice is not yet in vogue. The present study is expected to throw light on the attitudes of people in these two districts towards son preference and female foeticide. The sample drawn from Ernakulam and Malappuram selected from the central and northern regions respectively with quite different socio cultural milieu provides a representative sample of the heterogeneous Kerala Society.

6

Facts Unveiled

The data collected was subjected to percentage analysis and Chi- square test for independence of attributes as required by the hypotheses formulated for the study. The hypotheses were:

1. Strong son preference exists in the Kerala society as per the total sample and the relevant sub samples formed on the basis of gender, locale, religion, education and income levels.

2. There will be significant association of the response pattern to existence of son preference in Kerala society and the classificatory variables viz. gender, locale, religion, education and income levels.

3. There will be significant difference in the attitude towards female foeticide of people belonging to the different sub samples formed on the basis of gender, locale, religion, education and income levels.

4. There will be significant difference in the reasons attributed for son preference among people belonging to

different sub samples formed on the basis of gender, locale, religion, education and income levels.

Statistical Analysis of the Data

As per the hypotheses of the study percentage analysis was used to examine whether son preference exists in the sample and chi square test for independence of attributes was employed to examine whether there is any association between the dependent variable 'son preference' and the following classificatory variables:

(1) Gender of the respondents
(2) Locale of the respondents
(3) Religion of the respondents
(4) Level of education and
(5) Level of income

The results of the analysis are discussed below:

1. ASSESSING THE EXISTENCE OF SON PREFERENCE IN KERALA

1(a) Assessing the Existence of Son Preference in Kerala as per the Total Sample and Sub- samples Based on Gender and Locale

The existence of son preference in Kerala as per the sample was assessed using percentage analysis. The number of responses agreeing to the existence of son preference in Kerala society

TABLE 10

Percentage of Responses Agreeing to Son Preference in the Total Sample and the Sub-samples Based on Gender and Locale

Variable	*Sample Size*	*Those Agreeing to Son Preference*	*Percentage*
Total	450	316	70.2
Men	225	152	67.6
Women	225	164	72.6
Urban	230	176	76.5
Rural	220	140	64

was counted for the total sample and the sub-samples formed on the basis of the classificatory variables viz., gender, locale, religion, education and income levels. More than seventy percent of the respondents agreed upon that strong son preference exist in the Kerala society. The percentage of responses in the total sample and the sub-samples formed on the basis of gender and locale are given in Table 10.

Table 10 shows that 70.2 percent of the total sample agreed to the presence of son preference in Kerala society. 67.6 percent of men and 72.6 percent of women felt the existence of son preference. Among the urban sample 76.5 percent and among the rural sample 64 percent agreed to the existence of son preference in Kerala society. The pictorial representation of the findings is given in Figure 3.

FIGURE 3

Bar Diagram Showing Response to Existence of Son Preference by the Sub-samples Based on Gender and Locale

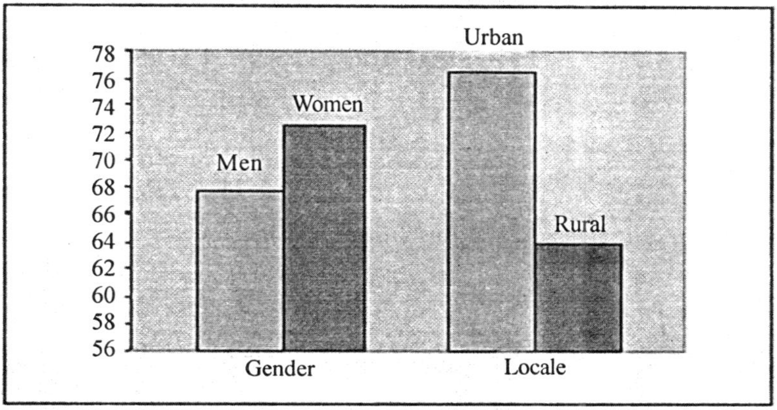

1(b) Assessing the Existence of Son Preference in Kerala as per the Sub- samples Based on Religion.

The percentage of response among the three major religious communities viz; Christians, Hindus and Muslims agreeing to the presence of son preference in Kerala society is given in Table 11.

TABLE 11

Percentage of Responses Agreeing to Son Preference in the Total Sample and the Sub-samples Based on Religion

Variable	*Sample Size*	*Those Agreeing to Son Preference*	*Percentage*
Christian	150	115	76.7
Hindu	150	106	70.7
Muslim	150	95	63.3
Total	450	316	70.2

As per Table 11 more than 60 percent of all the religious communities agree that son preference exists in Kerala society.

FIGURE 4

Bar Diagram Showing Response to Existence of Son Preference in the Sub-samples Based on Religion

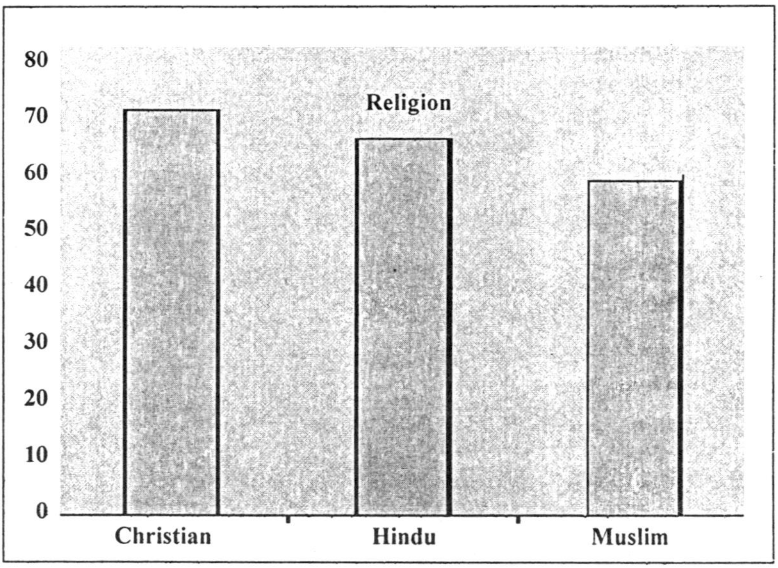

While 76.7 percent of Christians and 70.7 percent of Hindus agreed to the presence of son preference, respondents from the Muslim community showed the lowest percent of agreeableness with the existence of son preference in Kerala society. The pictorial representation is given in Fig. 4.

TABLE 12

Percentage of Responses Agreeing to Son Preference Based on Education Levels

Variable	*Sample Size*	*Those Agreeing to Son Preference*	*Percentage*
High	162	124	76.5
Average	180	126	70
Low	108	66	61.1
Total	450	316	70.2

FIGURE 5

Bar Diagram Showing Response to Existence of Son Preference in the Sub-samples Based on Level of Education

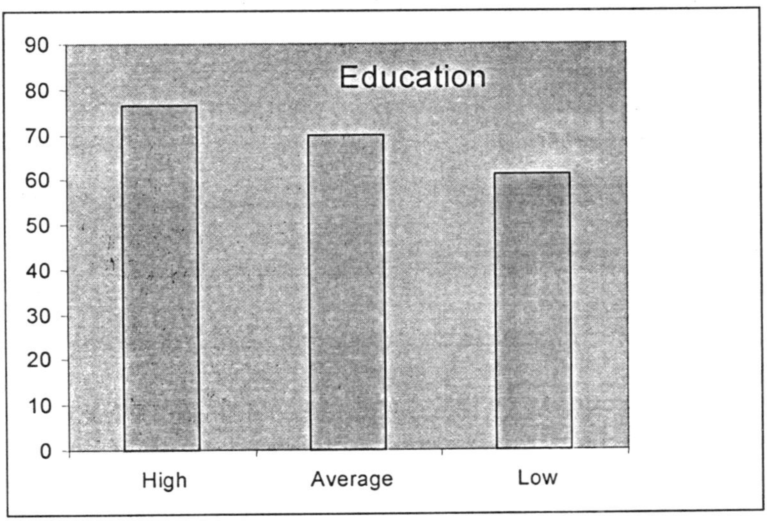

1(c) Assessing the Existence of Son Preference in Kerala as per the Sub- samples Based on Level of Education.

The percentage of responses showing agreeableness to the existence of son preference in Kerala society among the High-, Average- and Low Education groups of the sample are given in Table 12.

Table 12 shows that 75.5 percent of the High Education group of the sample agreed to the existence of son preference whereas 70 and 61.1 percent of the Average– and Low Education groups showed their agreeableness to the existence of the discriminatory practice in Kerala society. The pictorial representation of the above findings is given Fig. 5.

1(d) Assessing the Existence of Son Preference in Kerala as per the Sub- samples Based on Level of Income

The percentage of responses of people belonging to the three levels of income viz. High-, Average- and Low Income groups to the existence of son preference in Kerala society is given in Table 13.

TABLE 13
Percentage of Responses Agreeing to Son Preference Based on Income Levels

Variable	*Sample Size*	*Those Agreeing to Son Preference*	*Percentage*
High	132	108	81.8
Average	168	120	71.4
Low	150	88	58.7
Total	450	316	70.2

As per Table 13, the High Income group showed the highest of 81.8 percent agreeableness to the presence of son preference while the Low Income group showed the lowest percent of 58.7. Among the Average Income group 71.4 percent agreed to the existence of the phenomenon.

FIGURE 6

Bar Diagram Showing Response to Existence of Son Preference in the Sub-samples Based on Income Levels

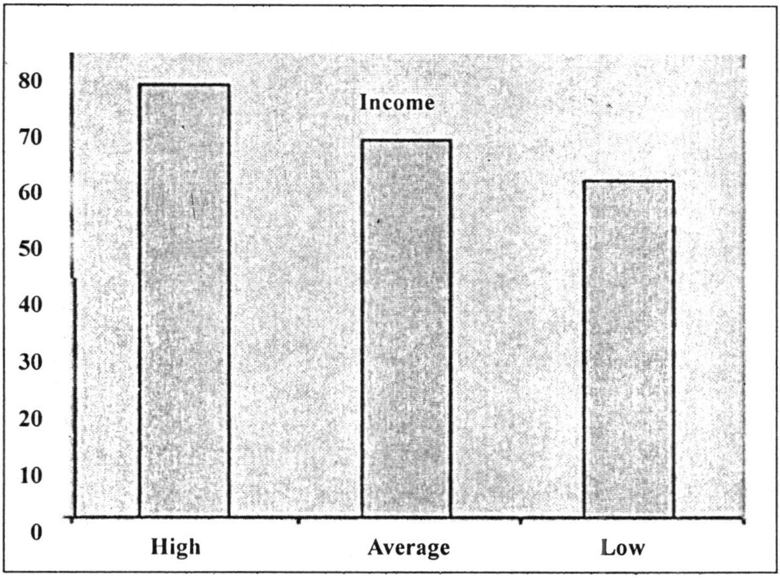

2. ESTIMATION OF THE ASSOCIATION BETWEEN THE CLASSIFICATORY VARIABLES AND THE RESPONSE PATTERN TO EXISTENCE OF SON PREFERENCE.

2(a) Association of Gender and Response Pattern to the Existence of Son Preference

The total sample consists of an equal number of men and women. Chi-square test for independence of attributes was attempted to estimate whether gender difference has an association with the nature of responses to the existence of son preference in Kerala society. It was found that gender difference of the sample does not have any association with the response given to the existence of son preference in Kerala society. Both men and women show similarity in their responses to the existence of the phenomenon without significant difference in their proportions.

2(b) Association of Locale and Response Pattern to the Existence of Son Preference.

The total sample was classified into two groups based on their locale viz., Urban and Rural. There were 230 urban and 220 rural subjects. These responses were subjected to the Chi-square test of independence of attributes to find out the association of locale and pattern of response to the existence of son preference in Kerala society.

Results of the test revealed a significant association between response given to existence of son preference and locale. 76.5 percent of urban subjects show agreeableness to the existence of the discriminatory practice in society whereas only 63.6 percent of the rural subjects expressed agreeableness.

2(c) Association of Religion and Response Pattern to the Existence of Son Preference

Chi square analysis of the data showed that the response pattern to the existence of son preference in Kerala society varies with the religious community. 76.7 percent of the Christian community shows agreeableness whereas 63.3 percent of Muslim community agrees to the presence of the discriminatory practice in the Kerala society.

2(d) Association of Levels of Education and Response Pattern to the Existence of Son Preference

The total sample is divided into three sub samples based on their level of education. The High-, Average- and Low Education groups consist of 162,180 and 108 individuals respectively. The responses regarding existence of son preference in Kerala society given by the three groups were subjected to Chi-square test of independence. A significant association between the level of education and response pattern to existence of son preference at 0.05 level was found in the analysis of data. 76.5 percent and 70 percent respectively of the High Education and Average Education groups show agreeableness to the existence of son preference whereas only 61.1 percent of the Low Education group agreed to it.

2 (e) Association of Level of Income and Response Pattern to the Existence of Son Preference

The total sample is divided into three sub samples on the basis of monthly income. They are High-, Average – and Low Income groups. The responses to the existence of son preference given by the three income groups were subjected to Chi-square test for independence of attributes in order to estimate the association between income level and response pattern. The results indicated the probability of strong association between income level and response to existence of son preference. Agreeableness to the phenomenon of son preference is shown by 81.8 percent of the High Income group while only 58.7 percent of the Low Income group reported the existence of the phenomenon.

3. COMPARISON OF ATTITUDE TOWARDS FEMALE FOETICIDE BETWEEN PEOPLE BELONGING TO THE TWO SELECTED DISTRICTS FOR THE TOTAL SAMPLE AND THE RELEVANT SUB-SAMPLES

The attitude towards female foeticide was assessed using a single item in the inventory, viz., **'What is your opinion about female foeticide'?**

The three possible responses were:

1. **It is to be condemned**
2. **It may be permitted if the situation demands and**
3. **There is nothing wrong with it.**

The response pattern to the above items was found to be much similar in the two samples each being drawn from the two districts. Out of the 450 respondents only 19 members opined that they do not consider female foeticide as a wrong doing. Fourteen of them belong to Malappuram district and five to Ernakulam district. Twelve of these respondents belong to low income families with low education levels. The rest seven including professionals and graduates belong to average income families. Only 6 members of the total sample responded that female foeticide may be done if the situation demands. The results are summarized in Table 14.

TABLE 14
Attitude Towards Female Foeticide as Indicated by the Samples Belonging to Ernakulam and Malappuram Districts

Sl. No	*Response*	*Ernakulam*	*Malappuram*	*Total*
1.	It is to be condemned	216	209	425
2.	It may be done if the situation demands	4	2	6
3.	There is nothing wrong with it	5	14	19
	Total	225	225	450

Since more than ninety percent of the sample had a negative attitude towards female foeticide, further analysis with regard to the various classificatory variables was not attempted. It was concluded that there is no significant difference in the attitude towards female foeticide of people belonging to the various sub samples formed on the basis of gender, locale, religion, education and income levels.

4. ANALYSIS OF THE MAJOR REASONS FOR SON PREFERENCE

The major reasons attributed to son preference existing in the society was analyzed for the total sample and the sub samples formed on the basis of the classificatory variables, viz., gender, locale, religion, education and income levels. **Three**

among the 10 plausible reasons given in the inventory were ranked No. 1 by majority of the respondents as the most plausible reason. They are the following:

1. **Economic burden necessitated by dowry to girl.**
2. **Belief that a son would carry on the family lineage.**
3. **Insecurity experienced by girl child in the society.**

Other reasons like a son would take care of parents during their old age, a boy would bring in financial gains to the family, birth of son would add to the social status of the family, life of girl child is disastrous when compared to a boy were also ranked as prominent reasons by a few respondents. There was much similarly in the responses irrespective of the gender, locale, religion, education and income levels of the respondents.

4(a) Major Reasons for Son Preference Attributed by the Total Sample and Sub-samples Based on Gender and Locale

The major reasons and the number of respondents who assigned Rank No. 1 for them in the total sample and the sub samples based on gender and locale are given in Table 15.

TABLE 15

Major Reasons for Son Preference as per the Total Sample and Sub -samples Based on Gender and Locale

Sl. No.	*Major Reasons*	*Men*	*Women*	*Urban*	*Rural*	*Total*
1.	Economic burden necessitated by dowry to girl	127	130	127	130	257
2.	A son would carry on the family lineage	32	27	29	30	59
3.	Insecurity experienced by girl child	22	32	30	24	54
4.	Other reasons	44	36	44	36	80
	Total	225	225	230	220	450

As evident from Table 15 the reason 'Economic burden necessitated by dowry to girl' was ranked as the most prominent reason for son preference in Kerala society by majority of the respondents. The proportion of respondents in the sub-samples based on gender and locale was found to be approximately the same with regard to the attribution of reasons. The next prominent reason was the belief that 'A son would carry on the family lineage'. In this case also almost similar number of responses was found in the sub samples based on gender and locale. The third prominent reason of 'Insecurity experienced by girl child' was also reported by similar proportions of the sub samples.

Even though Chi-square test was attempted to find out the association between plausible reasons and gender, no significant association was obtained. Similarly the Chi-square value for association between locale and the plausible reasons was also found to be negligent.

4(b) Major Reasons for Son Preference Attributed by the Three Major Religious Groups

The major reasons and the number of respondents attributing the same among the three major religious communities viz. Christians, Hindus and Muslims are given in Table 16.

Table 16 shows that the number of responses to the three major reasons shows much similarity among the three religious communities. Majority of respondents among Christians, Hindus and Muslims attribute Economic liability necessitated by dowry as the most prominent reason for son preference. In the case of other prominent reason also, the proportion do not show much variation. With regard to the reasons leading to the discriminatory practice, members of all religious communities have a common ground.

TABLE 16
Major Reasons for Son Preference Attributed by the Three Major Religious Groups

Sl. No.	*Major Reasons*	*Number of Religion-wise Respondents*			*Total*
		Christian	*Hindu*	*Muslim*	
1.	Economic burden necessitated by dowry to girl	83	83	91	257
2.	A son would carry on the family lineage	24	22	13	59
3.	Insecurity experienced by girl child	19	20	15	54
4.	Other reasons	24	25	31	80
	Total	150	150	150	450

The Chi-square value of test for independence of attributes was found to be negligent indicating a lack of association between religion and reason for son preference.

4(c) Major Reasons for Son Preference Attributed by the Three Educational Groups

The major reasons attributed to son preference in the Kerala society by the subgroups formed on the basis of education levels were also analyzed. The High -, Average-, and Low education groups were found to have much similarity in their responses to the major reasons for son preference. The number of responses given by the three subgroups formed on the basis of education level is given in Table 17.

Table 17 reveals that the proportion of responses of the three groups formed on the basis of education levels are much similar. In all the three groups, the majority of responses were favoring the reason economic liability necessitated by dowry as responsible for son preference.

TABLE 17

Major Reason for Son Preference Attributed by the Three Educational Groups

Sl. No.	*Major reasons*	*Number of Responses*			*Total*
		High Education	*Average Education*	*Low Education*	
1.	Economic burden necessitated by dowry	88	102	67	257
2.	A son carry family lineage	15	32	12	59
3.	Insecurity of girls	22	19	13	54
4.	Other reasons	37	27	16	80
	Total	162	180	108	450

The Chi-square value for association between level of education and reasons given for son preference was found not to be significant.

4 (d) Major Reasons for Son Preference Attributed by the Three Income Groups

The responses to major reasons for son preference attributed by the three income groups viz., High-, Average- and Low – income groups are given in Table 18.

TABLE 18

Major Reasons for Son Preference Attributed by the Three Income Groups

Sl. No.	*Major Reasons*	*Number of Responses*			*Total*
		High Income	*Average Income*	*Low Income*	
1.	Economic burden necessitated by dowry	72	99	86	257
2.	A son carry family lineage	27	16	16	59

(Contd.)

(Contd. Table 18)

Sl. No.	*Major Reasons*	*Number of Responses* High Income	Average Income	Low Income	*Total*
3.	Insecurity of girls	15	22	17	54
4.	Other reasons	18	31	31	80
	Total	132	168	150	450

As evident from Table 18 the proportion of responses to the major reasons for son preference among the three income groups show considerable similarity. Economic liability necessitated by dowry was attributed as the most prominent reason by majority of respondents in all the three income groups. The proportion of responses to other major reasons also shows much congruence.

Even though Chi-square test was attempted to find out the association between plausible reasons and levels of income, no significant association was obtained.

Discussion

The findings of the present study reveal the existence of son preference in the Kerala society. More than 70 percent of the total sample and more than 60 percent of all the sub samples based on gender, locale, religion, education and income levels agree to the existence of son preference. The only exception to this is found in the case of the Low-income group where 58.7 percent expressed their agreeableness to the existence of the phenomenon. The results of the study are in agreement with that of Patel (2003) and the NFHS-II Survey (1998-99) according to which Kerala had second position next to Andhra Pradesh among the southern states with regard to son preference. Research findings of Sulaja (2005) also substantiate this fact but according to her even though son preference exists in Kerala it is not that much crucial as in Karnataka or Tamil Nadu. But the Census details of 2001 especially of the 0-6 age group and the findings of the present study point to a crucial situation taking shape in Kerala too.

Estimation of the association of the classificatory variables and the response pattern to existence of son preference reveals interesting results. Though the response pattern was found to be independent of gender, strong association was found with locale, religion, education and income levels. The 'First Report on Religion Data, 2001' reveals the highest overall sex ratio of 1009 and the comparatively better child sex ratio of 964 for Christians among the various religious communities. But as per the present study highest percentage of respondents who expressed agreeableness to the existence of son preference in Kerala belongs to Christian community. Nevertheless, the mere agreeableness to the existence of a phenomenon in the society does not imply that the Christian community does have strong son preference. The finding that education and income levels may have an association with the response pattern to the existence of son preference has been revealed by several studies. As per the findings of the Centre for Social Research (The Hindu, 2005), preference for male child seems to be higher among the educated and rich sections of the society. In the prosperous and educated south Delhi Zone, the girl-boy sex ratio below five years has declined to 762 girls. Anyhow the association between education and income levels and the response pattern to the phenomenon of son preference in the present study does not warrant that the concerned education or income groups do have son preference. Perhaps the High-education and High-income groups might be more aware of the discriminatory practice existing in the society. But the findings of the association revealed between the attributes in other studies indicate the possibility of such an association in the Kerala society also.

Comparison of the attitude towards female foeticide of people belonging to Ernakulam and Malappuram districts reveals that while 5 respondents from Ernakulam do not consider female foeticide as a crime, the number of respondents from Malappuram showing a similar response is 14. Actually, the people from Ernakulam who enjoy the fruits of globalization in a better way with higher educational standards, more know-how and access to biomedical technologies were supposed to show more agreeableness with female foeticide. However, the findings suggest people of Malappuram, to be more in favor of female foeticide. Modernization and changing lifestyles by gulf migration and foreign remittances might have had an influence on the outlooks of people. In fact, such a trend might be the reason for doubling the gender gap in Malappuram in favour of male children during the period from 1991 to 2001 as evident from Table 4. Anyhow the percentage of respondents with positive attitude towards female foeticide in both districts is very low. Even though men and women do not show a blatant positive attitude towards female foeticide, the son preference believed to exist in the society might in turn have had an impact on the declining child sex ratio of the state. The strict adherence to small family norms (Mallik, 2002) coupled with easy availability of sex selection techniques and strong son preference points to the probability of female foeticide as a responsible factor for the missing girls. Findings of Agnivesh et al. (2005) also support the possibility of female foeticide among the rich and highly educated groups. Just as Patel (2002) opines threat of desertion, divorce and ill treatment also may force women to opt for sex determination and abortion in spite of their negative attitude to the evil practice.

Analysis of the reasons attributed to son preference shows an equal number of respondents favoring the prominent reasons and disfavoring the least plausible reasons. The three prominent reasons attributed were – 'Economic burden necessitated by dowry to girl', belief that 'A son would carry on the family lineage' and the anguish over 'Insecurity experienced by girl child'.

Other reasons like 'A son would take care of parents during old age', 'A boy would bring in financial gains to the family', 'Birth of son would add to the social status of the family', 'Life of girl child is disastrous when compared to that of a boy' were also ranked as prominent reasons by a few respondents. Gender, sex, religion, education and income levels were not found to have any influence on the reasons attributed to son preference. However the study pinpoints the crucial implications of the dowry menace which leads to the devaluation of the girl child threatening the very existence of the 'second sex'.

7

Case Studies

During the six months spent for data collection I have come across with a few friends whose experiences were so important in exposing the familial and social factors leading to son preference, along with the mental disposition of the women folk who are urged to undergo sex determination and abortion during their pregnancy period.

My interaction with Neena happened at the school where she is teaching as a guest lecturer in the plus two class. She is a post graduate from an affluent family. Her husband is a graduate business man from a rich family which has an obsession for sons. Neena belongs to a higher caste whereas her husband is from a relatively lower caste. When she became pregnant, the husband compelled her to go for scanning to which she objected on the grounds that it was their first child and even if it is a girl child she will not get it aborted. After a period of prayers and fasting, she gave birth to a girl child who she says was the end of all her happiness and beginning of all troubles. When she became pregnant afterwards, the husband threatened to kill her and their first child if she didn't go for abortion. The poor lady being jobless and helpless had to head to her husband's pressures and abort twice. Being a staunch Christian, she can't get out of the prick of conscience of having "killed" (in her own words) her children and is imposing lots of penance on herself by way of fasting, charity works and so on to get out of God's wrath on her. Her husband by the time has become a full time drunkard and she is blamed for his alcoholism on the grounds that he had wished for ten sons but she couldn't give him a single boy. Neena is prohibited from opening up the truth that she is not even allowed to carry her pregnancy to term. Later on she has undergone sterilisation Neena confines all her worries within herself just to keep up her family prestige. Today the father loves his daughter but blames the wife or humiliates her whenever they meet a young boy which Neena says happens every other day.

The meeting with Bindu was quite unexpected. She was an old friend of mine and I was explaining my whereabouts and recent engagement with the project. Bindu and her husband are happy couples of higher income group. Bindu's husband is a business magnet and both of them are highly educated. Bindu firmly believes that their happiness and higher status in society were due to their two sons for which she had to take some pains. Being settled in Bombay it was easy for her to undergo amniocentesis and get what they wanted twenty years back itself. When they got two sons Bindu underwent sterilization and both the parents believe that their timely decisions led to their happy and contented life with the two adolescent boys today. When asked whether they have any guilty feeling about what they have done Bindu jokingly said a stitch in time saves much time and money. So frank yet cool as in her college days, I wondered.....

Priya, a Hindu Ezhava girl is being continuously tortured by her mother in law with whom she stays back in Kerala while her husband is away in the gulf. It was her first pregnancy and her mother in law and sister in law used to harass her to go for scanning and determine the sex of the foetus. She says she was afraid of all such practices and used to pray a lot to beget a son. Unfortunately the child born was a girl. Since the birth of the child, she is been treated as a home maid with the minimum consideration of her higher educational status. The mother in law threatens the daughter in law to throw her out of the house if she ever happens to disclose the thing to anyone else. Priya confesses that very often she was tempted to kill the child and commit suicide. Her husband who is far off in the gulf turns up every alternate year and now at the age of 24, she is a mother of three children, the last one being a son. When asked whether her conditions improved with the birth of the son she said 'now my attitude has changed a lot and I know all these are part of life, I have to live for my kids'. The mother in law is happier these days but the price Resmi pays for her happiness is a life of slavery, suffering in silence and a sort of self alienation. With no permission to write letters, going out or making phone calls to husband, she seems to live a life of suspended animation.

My encounter with Sara was a different experience. Sara is a Muslim girl who got married recently at the age of twenty two. She is of the opinion that if the son is considered as a royal citizen of the society and if you have the choice of begetting one, why should the law or the women's movements object it. According to her the PNDT Act itself is discriminatory as it denies the human rights of a couple to have their own choice regarding procreation. She hopefully waits for three sons and for that she is ready to go for any measure as it is a prestige issue for her family which is famous for its fortune to have more of boys and very few number of girls. Being a postgraduate student she could be considered as a representative of the university student community with progressive attitudes, least bothered about values yet optimistic and confident of getting what they want.

Avila and her husband are higher secondary school teachers. They have a girl child of four years. They want to get a son next time. But Avila is afraid to conceive again since she is afraid of a repetition of her previous history. Being a Christian, she is afraid of sex determination and purposive abortion, which in turn might help them to have a son. She says that they had given a lot of offerings to churches during the first pregnancy but god didn't hear their prayers. Avila is in such a dilemma that she wants a son but is afraid of getting pregnant on the fear of begetting yet another girl child. Her husband encourages her to undergo sex determination next time by narrating the miraculous ways by which sons are born to his friends.

Nisha and her husband have three children –two elder girls and a younger boy. The family is reasonably well off and could afford any number of children. They love their daughters. She narrates the humiliation she had to face after the birth of each daughter and especially after that of the second daughter. She was all set to undergo any practice to get a son but not to give birth to yet another girl child. She underwent prenatal diagnosis for the purpose of sex selection which she resisted during the first three pregnancies. She explains how happy she and her husband, and the entire family of both of them had been when they came to know that this time she is conceiving a boy baby. Her younger daughter at the age of 12 years still now doesn't like to accept that she is a girl, instead she always wears boys' dresses and walk and talk like a boy. She takes much pride when commented to have a boyish look. The young child might have either experienced humiliation or have witnessed the way her mother is being humiliated for having given birth to daughters one after another. Nisha says that she was initially afraid of sex determination and considered it as a sin but the public itself made her bold enough to undergo scanning at any cost.

The experiences of the above young mothers reveal the motivation behind sex determination and the attitudes of the society, the immediate family, the husband and the woman herself towards foeticide. Most often it is the strong desire for a son irrespective of educational and economic standards of the family especially that of the husband or his immediate relatives that urges the woman resort to sex determination on a live or die principle. The prestige and happiness enjoyed by mothers having sons is also a tempting factor for several women. The humiliation and trauma through which a woman has to pass through after mothering a girl child is severe in the educated Kerala society too. In spite of their higher educational standards, people blindly blame the women for giving birth to daughters. Every pregnant woman of Kerala prays for a male child as a token of continued happiness, prestige and prosperity. In Kerala where strict small family norms are quite prevalent, begetting a son is considered as a matter of luck and fortune by the majority. The rich people have their own ways whereas the poor most often resort to prayers, offerings and pilgrimages. It could be concluded that the obsession to have a son with a small family size might be one of the factors responsible for the unfavorable child sex ratio in Kerala.

The bitter part of the story is that every young couple longs to have at least one son but is shy to confess their son preference openly. If the people of Mumbai or Punjab dare to reveal why and how they secured a son, the people of Kerala rarely do open up. May be their high standards of moral codes pressurise them to conceal the truth and wear the mask of nobility. In certain communities women consider themselves as cursed out of their inability to produce a son to light up the father's pyre and send him to moksha. As children, both boys and girls learn the basic principles of reproduction and how the sex chromosome from the father decides the sex of the child. But this education has nothing to do with wife blaming for not producing sons. The patriarchal values are internalised so deeply that even educated women who are heavily tortured by husband and in laws take up it as a normal reaction for her inability to conceive and deliver a son.

8

Government Programmes and Policies to Curb the Evil

A number of government programmes and policies including enactment of laws have been put forth to curb the evil of female foeticide. Several of them were the results of sustained campaign undertaken by women's rights activists belonging to different parts of the country. The major steps initiated by the government are given below.

1. Ban on Sex Determination Tests in Public Hospitals (1975-76)

During its introduction (1974) the All India Institute of Medical Sciences, New Delhi, initiated a clinical trial on the efficiency and acceptability of the prenatal diagnostic technology, amniocentesis. It was found that almost 90% of those who were part of the trial aborted the foetus if the procedure revealed the sex of the child to be female. Women's groups in Delhi were rightly concerned about this finding and immediately launched a protest to demand a ban on the use of these technologies for sex determination. The Government of India (GOI) responded by imposing a ban on sex determination tests in public hospitals.

The Ban imposed by the GOI on the availability of SD in public facilities was no doubt a positive step in the early stages of the introduction of diagnostic technology in the country. This Ban has directly resulted in the rapid commercialization and growth of the private sector for sex determination tests.

2. The Maharashtra Regulation of Prenatal Diagnostic Techniques Act, 1988

The Forum Against Sex Determination and Sex Pre-selection (FASDSP) initiated its campaign in Mumbai to raise awareness on SD and SSA and secure an effective ban during 1986 Earlier, during the early eighties, the issue involved just amniocentesis, now the pre-selection techniques was questioned. More over, although discrimination against women was a facet of the issue discussed, other concerns like misuse of technology and people's right to know and participate in decision-making in science and technology also became part of the general debate.

In this instance common ground was forged amongst groups ranging from the Young Women's Christian Association, NSUI (student's wing of the national Congress party), UNICEF, National Media Centre and the Humanist party. The main agenda of the campaign was the demand for a ban on SD. Although there was widespread support to the campaign amongst varied organizations as well as the media, it also had an equally large number of sceptics who considered the Forum's efforts as merely a magnification of what appeared to be a localized issue.

The FASDSP initiated its campaign in Mumbai to raise awareness on SD and SSA and secure an effective ban during 1986. Earlier, during the early eighties, the issue involved just amniocentesis, now the pre-selection techniques were questioned. More over, although discrimination against women was a facet of the issue discussed, other concerns like misuse of technology and people's right to know and participate in decision-making in science and technology also became part of the general debate.

As a result of the sustained campaign a new law was framed to ban SD and subsequently passed by the Maharashtra State Legislature titled the Maharashtra Regulation of Prenatal Diagnostic Techniques Act, 1988. This was later expanded in to a national level legislation titled the Pre-Natal Diagnostic Techniques (Regulation and Prevention of Misuse) Act (PNDT), 1994.

1. The Pre-Natal Diagnostic Techniques (Regulation and Prevention of Misuse) Act, 1994

The PNDT Act is a unique piece of legislation that not only guides the appropriate use of diagnostic technologies but also opened up space for articulating the need to regulate other types of reproductive and genetic technologies that were beginning to enter the Indian market. The objective of the Act was to 'provide for the regulation of the use of pre-natal diagnostic techniques for the purpose of detecting genetic or metabolic disorders or chromosomal abnormalities or certain congenital malformations or sex linked disorders and for the prevention of the misuse of such techniques for the purpose of pre-natal sex determination leading to female feticide' (MOHFW; 1994). The law had the dual objective of regulation of prenatal diagnostic technologies and prevention of misuse of these technologies for sex determination.

Some of the regulatory mechanisms include registration of genetic counseling centres, laboratories and clinics as well as the equipment used for performing the tests. Additionally, clinics were also mandated to employ personnel with a minimum skill base as prescribed by law. The Act also stated that even if the practitioner is fully qualified she cannot conduct a test or procedure in an unregistered site.

The Act also frames rules that regulate the terms of use of prenatal diagnostic techniques. A list of medical conditions is outlined, the existence of one or more of which is deemed to justify the recommendation for a pregnant woman to undergo pre-natal diagnosis. Where the test is being provided, written and informed consent from women undergoing the test has also been mandated.

Guidelines for Provision of Prenatal Diagnosis

The age of the pregnant woman is above thirty-five years.

The pregnant woman has undergone two or more abortions or foetal loss.

The pregnant woman has been exposed to potentially teratogenic agents such as drugs, radiation, infection or chemicals.

The pregnant woman has a family history of mental retardation or physical deformities or any other genetic disease.

Any other condition that may be specified by the Central Supervisory Board.

A number of institutional mechanisms have been outlined to ensure effective implementation of the law and in particular to prevent misuse of diagnostic technologies. The Central Supervisory Board (CSB) is a national-level body with high-ranking officials from both the Central and State governments, members of Parliament, eminent scientists and representatives of women's NGO's. The role of the Board was to advise the government on policy matters related to implementation of the PNDT Act, review implementation as well as recommend changes to the Act. The Central Supervisory Board has also been assigned the role of raising public awareness on the issue as well as specifying code(s) of conduct for personnel in genetic clinics.

At the state-level the Act included provision for the establishment of an Appropriate Authority (AA) as well as an Advisory Committee. Both these bodies to be appointed by the state government have as their main function the registration of genetic clinics as well as enforcement of standards for clinic conduct. AA's have also been empowered to investigate complaints against clinics as well as individual doctors. Some have critiqued the prominent and central role assigned to AA's as being too cumbersome as well as stifling individual initiative while investigating any type of misconduct or malpractice by a clinic or doctor.

The task of regulation of prenatal diagnostic technologies through Universal registration of clinics, equipment and licensing of practitioners was easier to enforce compared to implementing a complete ban on using the approved technology for sex determination. Registration of clinics while important cannot in itself prevent misuse of these technologies, particularly in the case of ultrasound where the sex of the foetus can be easily detected and communicated through verbal or other gestures leaving no visible marks on the woman's body.

An important provision of the PNDT Act was to prohibit advertisements that publicize technologies for SD or advertise clinics where the tests are available by making any violation of the prohibition a punishable offence.

A brief analysis of the PNDT Act 1994, serves to highlight some of the strengths as well as weaknesses that guide this unique effort to legislate the medical use of reproductive and genetic technologies on the one hand, and on the other, impose a ban on their non-medical use for sex determination. Key areas of critique have focused on the fact that in adopting the route of registration of clinics and equipment the law ends up sanctioning the private industry that has sprung up around provision of sex determination under the guise of pregnancy screening. Registration could well serve to legitimize these clinics as having a stamp of approval but it might not be effective in monitoring misuse or misconduct. Another critique has been the short-term view the law has taken with regard to NRTs limiting it to include ultrasound, CVS and amniocentesis, all technologies for SD. However, even as this law was being debated new pre-implantation (PGD) and preconception technologies were being introduced in the country by doctors trained abroad as well as manufacturers who considered India to be a good market to promote these technologies and harvest profits. As a result of this limited definition of the technologies that were included in the PNDT Act, 1994. Lingam (1998) points out that the law almost immediately appeared obsolete.

4. Public Interest Litigation by Dr. Sabu George, MASUM & CEHAT, 2000

Dr. Sabu George, Centre for Enquiry into Health and Allied Themes (CEHAT) and the Mahila Sarvangeen Utkarsh Mandal (MASUM) filed the PIL on SD in the Supreme Court of India in February 2000. The original petition provided evidence to validate claims that the PNDT Act, 1994, had failed to achieve its goals. The PIL also urged the Court to allow for an amendment to the Act that would allow for the inclusion of new techniques such as pre-implantation genetic diagnosis (PGD) and other pre-conception techniques for sex. selection.

In response to the Writ Petition, the Supreme Court issued notices to both the Central and State governments to file a response (5th May 2000). The States took almost a year to file their affidavits and soon after an interim judgment was delivered by the Supreme Court on 4 May 2001. The Court expressed strong concern about the non-implementation of the PNDT Act, 1994. The judgement included directives to the GOI and state governments to immediately activate the supervisory board in charge of implementation of the PNDT Act at the national level, Central Supervisory Board (CSB), as well as the state-level authorities. Regular half-yearly meetings till then not a regular feature of the CSB were ordered. The CSB was also given the mandate to examine the necessity of amending the existing Act-a demand made in the petition, mainly in recognition of the fact that new technologies that could be used for sex selection were becoming available in the Indian market and needed to be brought under the purview of the Act.

On 11 December 2001 the Supreme Court of India issued a second order directing five multinational companies-Philips, Symonds, Toshiba, Larsen and Toubro and Wipro GE- to give the name and addresses of the clinics and persons to whom machines had been sold during a five years period, 1996-2001. The objective neither was to provide State governments a list that would make it easier for them to track down individuals and clinics and in particular allow confiscation of equipment that was not registered and therefore their possession deemed illegal. As of February 2002, different companies had provided over 11,000 names to the Court. The Court also asked the medical association to provide lists of members who used ultrasound machines.

5. The PNDT Act (Legal Prohibition of Sex Determination) 2003

The amended version of the Pre-Natal Diagnostic Techniques Act, 1994, termed as the Preconception and Pre-Natal Diagnostic Techniques (Prohibition of sex selection) Act, was implemented in 2003. The Act provides for the prohibition of sex selection, before or after conception. As per the Act, the guidelines for registration of ultrasound facilities, their duties and obligations prohibit anyone connected with genetic laboratories, ultrasound clinics or imaging centers to associate with or help in carrying out the detection or disclosure of sex of the foetus in any manner. Every single detail concerning the pregnant woman has to be recorded, leaving no scope for loopholes. Detailed documentation has to be despatched at specific intervals to the prescribed authorities. **Through the 'Form F', the following vital information can be obtained:**

1. ***Number of children with sex of each child.***

2. ***Purpose for which ultrasound was done during pregnancy.***

3. ***Result of ultrasonography-if any abnormality detected.***

4. ***Was MTP advised/conducted? – Date on which MTP carried out.***

5. ***Declaration of doctor that while conducting ultrasonography, he has neither detected nor disclosed the sex of the foetus to anybody in any manner.***

6. ***Declaration of the pregnant woman that by undergoing ultrasonography, she does not want to know the sex of the foetus.***

Under the Act the person who seeks help, for sex selection can face imprisonment for a period of 3 years and be required to pay a fine of Rs. 50,000. The State Medical Council can suspend the registration of the medical practitioner involved and, at the stage of conviction, remove his/ her name from the register of the Council.

Under this Act, each enforcement authority consists of an officer of the rank of a Joint Director of Health and Family Welfare (JDHFW) as the Chairperson, an independent woman representing women's organizations and an officer of the Law Department of the State Government concerned.

The PNDT Act does not completely ban pre-natal diagnostic techniques. It permits their use under certain conditions:

- If the age of the pregnant woman is above thirty-five.

- If there is a history of mental retardation or physical deformities such as spasticity or other genetic disease.
- If the pregnant woman is exposed to potentially teratogenic agents such as drugs, radiation, infection or chemicals.

Under the present law, the use of pre-natal tests is considered justifiable only for the detection of five types of abnormalities, chromosomal abnormalities, haemoglobinopathies, genetic metabolic disorders, sex-linked genetic diseases and other congenital abnormalities.

The government has taken a number of initiatives to implement the Pre-Conception and Pre-Natal Diagnostic Techniques Act (PC & PNDT) and to spread awareness on the issue through Information, Communication and Education (IEC). They include amendment of the PC & PNDT Act in 2003 to make it more comprehensive; more frequent visits of National Inspection and Monitoring Committee (NIMC); setting up of National Support and Monitoring Cell (NSMC); sensitization through Members of Parliament; publication of handbook on the Act; Annual Report on the Act; Frequently Asked Questions (FAQ); involvement of District Magistrate; launching of "Save the Girl Child" campaign etc.

6. Save the Girl Child Campaign, 2007

The Save the Girl Child Campaign is a community-led awareness campaign to prevent female foeticide by generating gender sensitivity to increase the value and improve the health of female child especially in villages where the sex ratios are particularly poor with a greater intensity and frequency.

The President, Smt. Pratibha Patil launched the Ministry of Health and Family Welfare's Signature campaign on "Save the Girl Child", by being the first signatory on 2nd October 2007. The national campaign was launched to make society aware of the declining girl to boy ratio in the 0-6 year age group. An otherwise very important medical checkup termed "the ultrasound scan" plays the crucial role in issuing the death sentence to the girl foetuses. Although the Indian government has made using ultrasound scans only for the purpose of establishing the gender of the future baby a punishable offense, business booms. Immoral business people offering ultrasound scans from back offices paired with the society's belief in the supremacy of the male over the female sex apparently makes it difficult for the legal system to punish perpetrators.

Addressing the national meeting on 'Save the Girl Child' in New Delhi in 2007, the Prime Minister Man Mohan Singh urged people to actively participate in the 'Save the Girl Child' campaign. According to him the empowerment of girl child must begin at our homes, in our families and communities. He exhorted the elected representatives to actively engage in the national campaign for saving the girl child. The Prime Minister also asked the ministry of health to focus on orienting the million plus elected representatives of the panchayats and urban local bodies and use them as the medium for fighting this practice.

9

Looking Forward

Son preference, preconceptional and prenatal diagnosis, female foeticide, female infanticide, neglect, and abuse of female children together form one continuum. While the former aspects of the continuum are active the latter ones are passive. Generally female infanticide is more common in rural areas while in urban areas, females are not even allowed to be born. There also seems to be a slight financial barrier. Those who are poor find it cheaper to kill their daughters after birth, while those who have the money go for sex selection tests followed by abortions.

We were hopeful that with the implementation of the amended PNDT Act 2003, which makes it mandatory to keep records and audits regarding the diagnostic tests done, it would be possible to curb sex selection and female foeticide largely. But one cannot deny the fact that the super specialty hospitals and diagnostic centers in the private sector work not for charity but for money. For their cravings the son preference of the society is a blessing that however strong the law may be, loopholes will be found out. Hence the diagnostic tests during pregnancy should be permitted only in government hospitals.

The best measure to check the evil is by enhancing the value of the girl child. Even the average Keralite has fallen prey to the luxuries of consumerism, which has led to a high cost of living. This has further necessitated the observance of not only 'small family' norms but also 'only child family' norms. At a time when the neighborhood families rejoice over the birth of their honorable male citizens it is quite natural that one may crave for begetting such a celebrity as their own. With a high value attributed to the son, is it not curbing the right of a couple to have a preferred child and enjoy the credit and status of it when we make an outcry for implementing the PNDT Act? What is required is enhancing the value and status of the girl child, which is the only panacea for the son mania existing in the society. We have to think in terms of providing more opportunities through more relaxations, incentives and reservations for the deprived sex both as child and adult to augment the process of women empowerment through education, employment and political power whereby daughters could be thought of as assets and not as liabilities.

Age-old beliefs of parents that a son would carry on family lineage and that he would add on to social status to the family could be corrected only through proper awareness campaigns. When the young girls rise up to the standard of adding fame and prestige to the family, such narrow minded attitudes are likely to vanish from the society.

Increased violence and trafficking of girls and women have generated feelings of insecurity to the extent that it has become a reason for son preference of the public. Measures to ensure security to girl children must be taken up on a war footing. Severe punishments should be given to the culprits of violence and harassment of women as a price for their uncontrolled animal instincts. More alertness on the part of police and other law enforcement machinery is needed for this. The 24-hour helpline with enough number of dedicated women police personnel to control harassment of women is to be implemented in all districts whereby our girls and women could walk without fear holding their heads high.

If the present status of the girl child continues, there is every possibility of the new mindsets like 'not to have children, not to have a second child when the first is a boy' etc. to permeate to all sections and all classes. Several of the educated couples of Kerala seem to have such a strong conviction for the only child. Here the amended PNDT Act, of course a step in the right direction, will have to succumb to the status of a scarecrow when the atrocities and social abnormalities due to lack of women come out of the Pandora's box in the future society.

Immediate steps like enhancing the status of girl child along with attempts to bring about attitudinal changes in people and strict implementation of the PNDT Act and other Acts ensuring social security to girls and women are to be taken to avoid the far reaching consequences that may be brought about by the masculinization of the young and feminization of the aged. Punjab (Patel, 2005) and Haryana (Gertrude, 2005) experiences due to shortage of women population should be a moral lesson for people all over the country and especially to the so called elite society which takes too much pride in its women development indices and apparently good sex ratio.

A collective action for making our girls self confident, self reliant and self directive in education, health, employment, legal and political sectors is the immediate need of the hour.

Suggestions for Improving Social Practices

Suggested measures for curtailing the evil practices such as son preference, sex determination and female foeticide are given under the following heads:

- Implementation of the PNDT Act

- Strict enforcement of laws protecting girls and women
- Enhancing the value of girl child
- Awareness programmes
- Involvement of religion
- Involvement of media

(A) Proper Implementation of the PNDT Act

We were hopeful that with the implementation of the amended PNDT Act 2003, which makes it mandatory to keep records and audits regarding the diagnostic tests done, it would be possible to curb sex selection and female foeticide largely. From the Morena experience it is clearly seen that form "F" is not maintained properly. The purpose of collecting information under form "F" is to follow-up scanned cases till the child birth, find sex ratio centre-wise and see (i) how many cases are aborted and (ii) how many cases remain untraced. There should be stringent penalty for clinics that are defaulters on maintaining the form. Medical audits need to be made mandatory and strictly enforced.

But one cannot deny the fact that the super specialty hospitals and diagnostic centers in the private sector work not for charity but for money. For their cravings the son preference of the society is a blessing that however strong the Act may be, loopholes will be found out. Hence, the diagnostic tests during pregnancy should be permitted only in government hospitals. Strict monitoring of the activities of commercial minded techno-docs thriving on sexist prejudices should be effectively carried out with the help of social policing.

The fact that the amended PNDT Act is a cognizable, non bailable and compoundable offence, such that the offender may be arrested without warrant needs to be widely publicized.

Vigilant bodies of concerned citizens must be mobilized to be proactively involved. The Right to Information Act can provide teeth to the local level organizations in this regard.

(B) Strict Enforcement of Laws Protecting Girls and Women

Increased violence and trafficking of girls and women have generated feelings of insecurity to the extent that it has become a reason for son preference of the public. Measures to ensure security to girl children must be taken up on a war footing. Severe punishments should be given to the culprits, of violence and harassment of women, as a price for their uncontrolled animal instincts. More alertness on the part of police and other law enforcement machinery is needed for this. The 24-hour helpline with enough number of dedicated women police personnel to control harassment of women is to be implemented in all districts whereby our girls and women could walk without fear holding their heads high.

(C) Enhancing the Value of Girl Child

The best measure to check the evil is by enhancing the value of the girl child. Even the average Keralite has fallen prey to the luxuries of consumerism which has led to a high cost of living. This has further necessitated the observance of not only 'small family' norms but also 'only child family' norms. Proactive role must be played by the National Women's Commission and the respective State Women's Commissions to look at policies that lead to societal female devaluation. Equal inheritance to ancestral property as well as equal remuneration for men and women need to be clearly examined.

Also we have to think in terms of providing more opportunities through more relaxations, incentives and reservations for the deprived sex both as child and adult. Such measures would augment the process of women empowerment through education, employment and political power whereby daughters could be thought of as assets and not as liabilities.

Programmes such as the 'only girl child scholarship' implemented by the CBSE are right steps in this direction.

Schemes in various states such as Haryana that give incentives to families where there is a daughter need to be promoted on all India level.

(D) Awareness Programmes

Age-old beliefs of parents that a son would carry on family lineage and that he would add on to social status to the family could be corrected only through proper awareness campaigns. When the young girls rise up to the standard of adding fame and prestige to the family, such narrow minded attitudes are likely to vanish from the society. What is needed most is a change in mindset of doctors and clients, to create a socio-cultural milieu that is conductive for girl child's survival.

(E) Involvement of Religion

In the present study a significant association was found between religion and the response pattern towards son preference. Campaigns at the grassroots level should be designed using religion as its aid. Religion should be used as a tool to spread the message, as today most communities are influenced by the dictates of religious organizations and spiritual leaders. The religious dimension of the issue needs special attention.

(F) Involvement of Media

The media most often depict a negative portrayal of women in traditional stereotypic roles which indirectly devalues womanhood. Images of women who are confident and active, economically independent, socially committed and politically conscious must be projected so that they would serve to enhance the dignity of women and create a positive image of women in human minds and hearts. The details of women's depiction in media, its consequences and the role to be played by media are all dealt in detail in chapter 10.

10

Enhancing the Status and Dignity of Girl Child

Enhancing the status and dignity of girl child is the most important and most effective step to curb the prevalent evils of son preference and female foeticide. As opined by one of the respondents in the project, 'how can you blame a couple going for available means to beget a son and get rid of an unwanted daughter when the son is so much valued in the society'. So long as a son is considered as a proud possession of its parents, a celebrity at home and in the society and so long as mothering a son is considered as a blessing, getting a son will remain an obsession to couples. What we need here is a shift in the focus from son to daughter. The major reason for son preference as revealed from the study is that 'a daughter is considered as a liability because of the dowry system'. This is a mentality that can be easily changed through enhancing the dignity of girl children. But how can one achieve this target. Let us look into Vanitha's life.

Vanitha's Example

The Book was started with the experience sharing of Vanitha and let us see how she got actually empowered before winding up the Book. Once she decided to live a life of her own, she started searching for her identity- her inborn strengths and weaknesses, her special abilities and why she is living a life on this earth. Her introspection in the hospital bed for three days helped her in finding answers to all such questions. Next she started thinking of a way out, without depending on others. As Vanitha opines, her brilliant academic record and the reinforcements she had received in her school and college days might have helped her in not succumbing herself to the cruel fate and withstanding the pressures and challenges that life has offered.

Vanitha explains how she had to take care of the unfortunate daughter and continue her higher studies without any financial or emotional support from anyone except her younger brother. She had to take a lot of pain to convince the husband and mother in law why she wants to study further. Even her own family people couldn't digest the idea of her further studies. Amidst the constant blame from relatives, she could succeed only because of her strong determination to become economically independent. She never bothered about the comments and blames, some of which were so cruel.... that 'her husband might have deserted Vanitha since he has extramarital affairs in Bhopal'...., 'though she is good at studies she might be an utter failure in satisfying her husband'...., 'she doesn't know how to be a good submissive wife'....., 'she might be divorced from her husband' and so on. She ignored all gossips but what was more cruel was the lack of money and lack of any supporting system. She had to stay at her own family, almost as one of the maid servants at her home....endure the insults by the sister in law, almost last and least fed..... .Her husband made phone calls once a while but was least interested to listen to her. Neither did he send a single rupee to her nor enquired about how she is getting along with the child.

She recollects how she had travelled in buses and trains with empty stomach to the college, how much she longed for sufficient money to have a cup of coffee in the train while the fellow travellers used to have their breakfast. Spending three rupees for a tea or coffee was a luxury that she couldn't imagine at that stage. Instead of hiring an autorikshaw she used to walk kilometers to reach home. While her classmates took photocopies of study materials, she had to sit late nights to write them up. Life became too horrible when the child fell ill at times. Without any money, it was quite impossible for her to consult a doctor. Her younger brother was kind enough to secretly provide the bare minimum to her without others noticing it. A voiceless and helpless Vanitha suffered everything in silence amidst humiliation and hatred from all corners for two years. She also recollects the trauma and humiliation, a married girl has to pass through if she happens to stay at parental home for more than a week or two. According to Vanitha, it was her strong determination for an independent life and true faith in God that gave her, the strength to withstand everything. At the end, her hard work was well paid of, she passed her exams with top ranks and distinction and by the time the results got published, she got an immediate placement. The economic independence made her more confident, bolder and stronger and she has never again gone to Bhopal.

Though life had its own pressures from various corners, things were quite easier this time. Again she pursued her part time studies and research, carried out projects, published her works and got engaged throughout the time. Meanwhile the husband became a frequent visitor of the rented home and started acknowledging her capacities and respecting her individuality. Vanitha was rising up in her career and the daughter was all around her as an unusually strong supporter in all her efforts. The diad, a model to all mothers and daughters, helped and supported each other and both of them were growing in every sense. Life has changed a lot and according to Vanitha, her daughter is so kind and generous to the poor and suffering as against her age mates since she herself had passed through such pathetic experiences in her childhood. Today the father has come back from Bhopal and they are living together, loving and sharing everything. When she set out for higher professional qualifications and secured a regular highly paid job, Vanitha's entire lifestyle changed.

Vanitha was a postgraduate at the time of marriage but was denied opportunities for permanent jobs and the little money she got from her contractual employment made her a slave of the husband. Her beauty and huge dowry at the time of marriage couldn't help her in anyway. She was least respected despite the postgraduate degree she had at the time. In Vanitha's opinion, this is what happens to majority of educated girls, the subjection and subjugation of female individuality to male chauvinism which gets manifested in one way or the other. Several case studies on Keralite women support Vanitha's reflections:

Broken Souls and Shattered Individualities

This title is the most suitable adjective for majority of Keralite women. One may come up with arguments highlighting the women development indices of Kerala. The indices are all true but what goes on behind the curtain is not known to the world outside. A few case studies conducted by the author to obtain a better insight into the problems of the so called educated Keralite women may help to reveal the hypocrisy of the elite.

Case 1

Mrs. M hailing from a very affluent family is married to a business magnet. Even after 8 years of marriage, they have no children and both of them are still under treatment for infertility. He is an alcoholic and once drunk all his moral restraints get out of control. Mrs. M is forced to accompany the husband as a status symbol in public meetings where she is often ridiculed. During one such incident, he pushed a full pack of tissue paper into her mouth when she attempted to stop him from drinking more. Though a post graduate, she is not free to seek an employment, as her husband fears that she would leave him on becoming independent. Mrs. M tries to contain her worries within herself in an attempt to protect her family's prestige. She hopes her husband would become normal once a child is born to them. A staunch christian, she firmly believes that her prayers would bring a positive change in her present life.

Case 2

Mrs. B, 38 years, young looking and attractive, has 2 children - elder daughter, 14 years and younger son, 6 years. Her husband, 45 years old, is a doctor and owns a private clinic. Both appearance-wise and caste-wise, they are at either extreme. The marital life was not smooth from the beginning when the husband started preventing the wife from maintaining ties with her own family members. Problems started precipitating when the man who did not show any sexual interest towards his wife for the last six years, suddenly started having an illicit relationship with a nursing staff staying back even at nights at the clinic. In addition, he resorted to other deviant acts such as locking up the wife and children in home and disconnecting facilities like telephone and air conditioner. His suspicious nature does not let Mrs. B to go out alone or seek a job. Instead, she is reduced to the status of a mere showpiece, just accompanying him for parties. The children distanced themselves from the father and hate him as he often threatens to kill the daughter. Mrs. B, because of economic necessity and for the sake of rearing the children, is living a life with her husband knowing that he is ignoring her physical and psychological needs. The thought of whether her husband has an eye on his daughter is also gnawing her. She thinks of divorce as a welcome solution, provided she and her children get financial aid from him.

Case 3

Mrs. S, 50 years old, is a college professor, and her husband is also in an equivalent position. Still, Mrs. S does not enjoy any financial independence as her husband maintains a tight control of her salary. She has no say not only in financial matters but also in family matters. A strict autocrat, he did not even allow his wife to invite her relatives and friends to the marriage ceremony of their only daughter. That was the last straw on the camel's back, and on the marriage eve, when her daughter left to the matrimonial home, Mrs. S exploded, unleashing her pathetic life of no freedom, much to the surprise of the public. It came as a shock even to the closest relatives to sense what was beneath the mask. Mrs. S does not want to prolong her suffering, now that her daughter is happily married off.

Case 4

Mrs. L, a post-graduate, the only daughter of rich Hindu Nair parents was married to a rich businessman. Unfortunately his sexual perversions were beyond her tolerance limits. Her problems started cropping up after the birth of their only daughter. The husband appeared extremely loving of his wife to others. That it was just as veneer became clear when she disclosed that is was his suspicious nature that was behind his considerate looks. With adequate emotional and social support from her family, Mr. L divorced her relation with him and was fortunate enough to obtain a prestigious job.

Case 5

Mrs. R is the wife of a high class, may be one among the richest of the state, executive with elegant looks and charming personality. She is a graduate and of course very beautiful, noble, gentle, happy young lady in her looks. Almost all women, belonging to the various clubs of the city might have envied at her glittering costumes and jewellery. But she is a totally shattered wife within the four walls of her home. The husband travels a lot, international tours very often, comes back and insist the wife to listen to his detailed 'so called adventurous experiences' with women in each country. She has to listen him attentively for maintaining the marriage, just for the sake of her adolescent daughters who are pursuing their professional studies. What worries her most is the way her husband brings home young girls, to their own bedroom while she has to wait outside. According to her, she is living a worthless life except for guarding the lives of the daughters. She repeatedly says that she will finish her life on the day when the younger daughter gets married off.

The few case studies described above reveal that all forms of domestic violence exist in the Kerala society irrespective of caste, religion, educational status and economic background. Majority of women live a life of suspended animation which accounts for the lowest mental health profiles of Keralite women. Even though they crave for a divorce from their 'masters', they can't do it due to their economic dependency on the husbands. The funny yet terrific fact behind the experiences shared is that all these women usually do have the attire of happy adorable wives which in their own words is a must to keep life going on. Otherwise the master would get offended and the consequences would get out of your control. Live an unhappy marriage without any opportunity to open up, yet act to be happy and contended with a smiling face is the fate of these broken souls. The years of silence on the face of violence and the learned hopefulness of women have not improved, but worsened their conditions. The domestic violence that previously existed in slums and poor families has now crept into the middle class and rich families of the state. The more educated ones are the civilized culprits who act as decent, gentle and caring husbands outside whereas they become so mean and cruel inside the homes. This doesn't mean that all men are bad and all women are angels in God's own country. But there is an alarming rise in the number of men bearing the hard core of indifference and chauvinistic attitudes towards women and the number of women who are getting their individualities shattered to such an extent that they can't even think of living a life with dignity. How can we come out of this tragic situation? How can we enhance the status and dignity of our girls and women?

Living a Life With Dignity

On several occasions this topic has become the thrust area for seminars and discussions. It is the human right of every individual, man and woman to live a life on this earth with dignity. But our women have developed mistaken identities that they fail to realize it as their right and they do not even think about such an issue. In consciousness raising classes for girls and women, the questions often asked and the answers followed are listed below:

Qn: Why does society show discrimination to girls?

Ans: Society doesn't know the value of girls.

Qn: Are girls equally good as boys?

Ans: Not only are they equally good, they are better than boys in various capacities.

Qn: Why do boys seem smarter and active than girls?

Ans: From the time a girl child is born, whatever is said and done in the name of socialization by its various agencies, knowingly or unknowingly, encourages the girl to be inactive, passive and dependent. It is quite difficult to make the girls unlearn this learned helplessness. But boys receive a different kind of socialisation which encourages them to be smart and active.

Qn: Why do parents socialise their boys and girls differently?

Ans: Parents always wish the best for their children whether they are boys or girls. But discrimination is practiced unknowingly and in certain cases knowingly even by educated parents because of a complex pattern of biases and belief systems existing in the society.

Qn: Can you suggest an example where a parent is pressurised to show discrimination against girl children?

Ans: There can be any number of examples. As per our customs and traditions, marriages are patrilocal and a girl is married off to boy's house. Parents cannot even think about their daughter being harassed by the husband's family for her being smart, active or talkative. So naturally, parents will insist on such behaviours in their daughter which seem to be pleasing and appropriate for a girl as per social expectations, like passive, silent, docile, being at service for others etc.

In yet another case, boys are allowed to go out for play while girls are not. Here, parents are too much anxious about the safety of girls which very often is something out of their control in the present social set up. So a parent naturally will put restriction on the mobility and social circle of girls.

Qn: So would you say to ensure safety of girls they are to be kept within the four walls of the home?

Ans: Never, girls have equal rights as boys to live a full life on this beautiful earth. But they should be made aware of the issues and problems in the society, their causes and remedial measures. They should be made aware of all means of self help, in case of problematic situations.

Qn: Men and women have different physique and mental disposition. So is it not natural that wifehood and motherhood are the goals of women's lives?

Ans: Of course, men and women are different in their physical qualities and capacities. But this does not mean that women should confine themselves within the homes for wifing and mothering. Wifehood and motherhood should be equated with husbandhood and fatherhood.

With regard to mental disposition men and women are equal. But the unequal socialisation and lack of opportunity for education and employment result in a kind of cumulative backwardness in sisters when compared to brothers even within the same family.

Qn: Will you please elaborate on this cumulative backwardness?

Ans: This can be easily compared with the backwardness faced by the socially and culturally unfortunate men and women.

For instance, a tribal boy however smart and intelligent he may be, lag behind because of his regional, social and cultural circumstances. Due to lack of sufficient and proper educational opportunities in the childhood he will be pulled down in higher classes even if given equal opportunities at the later stage. This cumulative backwardness gets deepened and strengthened as he moves into professional classes. That is why very often drop outs are seen among tribal students in professional colleges. If it is a girl she will be subject to double discrimination.

Due to the social notion that men are the breadwinners, parents give more priority for the education of boys than girls. The boy may be sent to private schools with higher fees whereas the girl will be sent to the nearby Government school with no fees. Again when it comes to higher education, majority of parents send their boys to professional education whereas their sisters will be sent to postgraduate courses in Arts and Science Colleges. This is true even in the departments of the Universities. The percentage of boys in MA/M.Sc classes in most departments is less than ten percent. More than 90 percentage of girls in such classes is a matter to be taken pride of but when we find answer to the question of "where gone are the boys", we will feel pity for ourselves. Boys are sent to high paid professional courses in prestigious institutions. When it comes to jobs, the professionally educated boys will get prestigious jobs when compared to girls who have completed the traditional courses.

Qn: Isn't there a change in the trend these days?

Ans: Yes, there is a slight change in the trend with more and more girls joining technical and professional courses and that provides a ray of hope. But this change happens only when the parents are educated and aware of the value of professional education. Majority of the population, in rural areas and in certain specific communities and regions still value marriage as a better option for ensuring the future safety of their daughters rather than sending them for professional education.

Such parents may send their daughters to postgraduate courses with a view to enhance their value in the marriage market and not as a means to enhance their employability.

Qn: Would you stress on professional education for girls whose parents are economically well off?

Ans: There is a wrong but popular notion that if the girl belongs to a rich family, the dowry demands can be easily met, to get a prosperous husband and hence she may not require any higher education. Such beliefs emphasize on one side the stereotypic roles of girls and women and on the other side under estimate the need for professional education to women. Whether rich or poor, as long as a girl is considered to be fit only for wifing and mothering, both of which are unproductive income wise, the demand for dowry will persist in the society. If the girl is to become a wage earner she must have either the necessary skill training or professional qualification.

Qn: What solution will you recommend for the emancipation of girls who are not in a position to go for professional education either due to economic, cultural, regional or physical constraints?

Ans: Economic, cultural and regional constraints very often merge with each other. For example, a tribal woman or a dalit woman usually happens to face all these deprivation simultaneously. Had these women been given an exposure to be brought up in a different world, for instance, by educated parents, their destinies would have been totally different. In the case of women who are marginalised and face cumulative backwardness and discrimination because of physical impairment or due to economic and cultural constraints as in the case of dalit women or regional, cultural and economic constraints as in the case of tribal women, special reservations and relaxations in education and employment is the best option. This is something that is being implemented today but not so satisfactorily or successfully. They must be given special attention and additional coaching from the early days onwards. Their parents must be provided proper awareness regarding the role of education in improving life situations which can be effectively taken up by the specific government machinery instituted for the purpose and by non – government agencies. Those girls who still fail to compete with the mainstream may be helped with vocational training and entrepreneurship training. They must be made aware of the method and merits of forming women cooperatives and SHG's to start entrepreneurship programmes. In one way or the other every girl must be helped to become economically independent.

Qn: Are you for special reservation and relaxations for women to promote their participation in the public sphere?

Ans: As I said earlier, women of today are facing the cruel reality of cumulative backwardness. One may highlight token success stories of women to prove that women do not need any reservation, what they need is gender equality only etc. Yes, there may be hundreds of women who have been fortunate enough to get support from their families and there may be yet another hundreds who might have had the strength and courage to overcome the learned helplessness and cumulative backwardness so as to become empowered themselves and lead successful lives. But the point to be specially noted here is that there are millions of women who fail to overcome their learned helplessness and cumulative backwardness. Coupled with this, the strong forces of oppression and discrimination pull down women from active participation in the public sphere including productive employment and political participation. It is not the lack of ability or willingness but it is a matter of lack of opportunities that make women lag behind. For example, there had been lot of apprehensions regarding how women are going to perform when 33 percent reservation was declared for women in the administrative set up of local self governments through the 73rd and 74th amendment acts. There had been a number of presentations that dealt with the effectiveness and problems faced by women elected representatives of local self governments in every seminar and conference on development in the latter part of ninetees. But after a decade you don't hear any such deliberations, as time has proved the efficiency of the so called second sex. Hence we are in a stage where special reservation should be ensured for women in all spheres of decision making. Reservation here is a matter of humanitarian consideration to give an opportunity to the deprived sections their due share. The next generation women brought up by parents and teachers who are aware of the need for gender justice and who do not practice gender discrimination, may not require any reservation. To prove themselves, the women of today must get support through reservation and relaxations in productive employment and political leadership in legislative assemblies and parliaments.

Yet another reason for reservation is the fact that gender discrimination in the patriarchal society denies women their due share in decision making bodies. Until a change in mindsets happen, to admit and accept women as equal partners, this denial is likely to continue. For example, you take the case of members in decision making bodies of higher education institutions like the number of women Vice Chancellors, Registrars, Pro-vice Chancellors, Finance Officers etc. and the number of women members in the Syndicate, the Senate, the Academic Council and so on in the Indian Universities. It will be a highly disappointing minimum. Is it because we do not have talented and committed women academicians to take leadership roles? No, it is because women are purposefully denied their due share. If there is fifty percent reservation of such seats for women, definitely a lot of women will come forward and utilise the opportunity to prove their talents and enrich the academic world with their nurturing and protective visions.

Women need special relaxations in age and experience as has been practised in national level examinations (like NET/

JRF) and in employment opportunities. The career graph of men usually go straight while that of women shows several ups and downs. This is because of the familial responsibilities entrusted upon women for mothering and parenting and taking care of the aged at home. Of course, mothering is something that cannot be shared by anyone for which women have to pay a high price in the pursuit of higher studies and promotion chances in career. The steps taken by the government to provide 30 months maternity leave for women is a highly appreciable move to compensate this. But parenting and taking care of the aged are responsibilities to be shared on an equal basis by men and women. The move to provide paternity leave is a bold step in this regard both for generating awareness among men regarding their responsibility in equal parenting and to relieve the mothers of their burden of childcare along with self care during delivery and post partum period.

Qn: Would you elaborate on the concept of 'learned helplessness'?

Ans: As I said earlier girls are equally good as boys. But the improper socialisation which I would like to refer as a sinful act rendered by the family, educational institutions, media, religion and other agencies of socialisation make the girls internalise certain false notions about themselves such as they are incapable of several things that boys are capable of, they are tender, they are to be passive and dependants, they are to be protected and taken care of by men and so on. Finally girls imbibe this learned helplessness which is very hard to unlearn.

Qn: Would you advocate scholarship and reservation for girls in professional courses?

Ans: Definitely, because girls are deprived of their duc share in financial support and warmth from parents and social sanction to move around and learn together with peers. Parents are reluctant to send their daughters to professional courses in distant places out of fears regarding their safety which they very much will do with regard to their sons. Parents are also reluctant to extend financial support for girls in doing courses having high fee structure. But if girls are given reservation and scholarship, at least the genuinely interested ones may get an opportunity to pursue their higher studies despite the lack of willingness of parents on various grounds and ability of parents to afford it.

Qn: Is it okay that a girl remains as a housewife if her husband is rich enough and caring?

Ans: If a girl by herself opts to be a housewife, it can be admitted to a certain extent. But if a girl who used to excel in her studies and was ambitious of a career is compelled to remain as a housewife it is cruel. It will be a heavy blow on her personality, her desires and hopes which in turn might throw her into a state of depression.

Qn: Women of Kerala have the highest literacy and educational standards when compared to their counterparts in other states. But they are the highest consumers of antidepressants. How will you relate these two variables?

Ans: Keralite women have the lowest mental health profiles as per the estimates of the Indian Psychological Association. The low mental health of women in the glorified society has its roots in a clutch of factors including unequal power relations within the family, economic dependence of women, extreme materialistic outlook and pleasure seeking culture, alcoholism and personality disorders of husbands, increasing violence against women, negative portrayal of women's image in media and absence of adequate social support systems.

A major aspect to be related to this is the low economic participation of Keralite women which is much lower than the national average. I have come across hundreds of women who are highly educated and professionally qualified but have to contend themselves with their wife and mother roles. Most of them share their dissatisfaction with the lack of further accomplishments in life. So the compulsion to housewife role can be one of the reasons for the poor mental health of educated Keralite women.

Qn: Do you mean all employed women are contended and having good mental health?

Ans: Never, employment and economic independence would generally facilitate the empowerment of women. But there are a good number of women who are wage earners but having no control over their earnings. Such a condition will not contribute to sound mental health. More over the role conflicts of women with no power within their marriages are likely to be worse than that of others with decision making power.

Qn: Working women face lot of role conflicts. So why should be women encouraged taking up jobs?

Ans: There are several reasons. First and foremost, the uncountable potentials of millions of women have been wasted on this earth without being visible, recognized or utilized for national development. Secondly, if a woman is economically a versatile parasite, she can never claim an equal status with men. As long as she is dependent on others, she is treated as a slave at service of the provider and this very often aggravates her subjectivity to exploitation by the 'super sex'. The same feeling is reflected in the words of Jawaharlal Nehru when he opines 'freedom depends on economic conditions even more than political and if the woman is not economically free and self-earning she will have to depend on her husband or someone else and dependants are never free'. Thus economic independence is an essential aspect that is to be ensured for enhancing the dignity of girl children.

Qn: Your suggestions for minimising the role conflicts of women?

Ans: The best solution is equal sharing of household chores by husband and wife. Similarly equal parenting and sharing of old age care will relieve women from their role conflicts to a great extent. Nuclear families can go for other social support systems like crèches and day care centres of the aged whenever needed. Implementing governmental initiatives for providing maternity and paternity leave to young parents both in the organised and unorganised sectors is a timely requirement in this regard.

Qn: Why do the concepts of equal parenting, equal sharing of household chores and equal caring of the aged fail to get acceptance and approval of the public?

Ans: The answer is simple, the inability of men and women to accept change. Whatever beliefs and notions that our men and women had been following and whatever activities they had been practising for the ages is not easy to be changed all of a sudden. As the patriarchal notions are so deeply imbibed due to socialisation, it requires continuous brainwashing of the unhealthy notions and refilling with progressive attitudes of the successive generations. Nobody can be blamed in this regard. What we see today is an encouraging trend where our youngsters are getting bold enough to accept change and practise equal sharing. May be the next generation will be totally different in their outlooks and practices provided the various agencies of socialisation like the educational institutions, religion and media support families in proper socialisation of children. Proper awareness creation for changing the mindsets of men and women is a task which needs comprehensive and synergic action by all these institutions.

Qn: You advocate employment of women as a norm. Who will take care of the aged when all women get employed?

Ans: Who said taking care of the aged is a women's responsibility? Why not men share it with women equally? Another possibility that requires serious concern and attention is our notions regarding old age care. Of course it is our responsibility to take care of the aged, our parents and all elders.

But it is high time we think about alternatives. In several cities there is a welcome move of providing day care facilities for the aged, where aged parents will be taken care of in a friendly, warm and healthy environment with medical and other supportive facilities. They get opportunities to discuss and share their feelings and experiences with age mates from various backgrounds along with quality care. This will create more employment opportunities for the youngsters on one side and on the other side enhance the employability of the educated girls who had been denied of the chance in the name of looking after the aged parents in their families. More and more of day care homes for the aged should be started in all cities and major towns.

Our notions regarding old age homes are also to be redefined. In an age of stiffer competition one cannot expect to get a suitable employment in the native town, state or country. In the global world, one should be ready to move with the tide to lead a satisfying life. If the children are not in a position to take the parents with them, parents should be ready to adjust with the situation. Here comes the need to change our perceptions regarding old age homes that they are not dumping yards of the aged, instead they are places of comfort and companionship with age mates, which the aged may be denied even when they are at home with children. The loneliness and alienation felt by thousands of aged parents in the 'so called' happy families noted for their parental care is a matter that needs to be studied scientifically. Our aged parents are not in a position to digest the notion of being cared by anyone other than own children. But it is high time that the second generation parents of today learn to reorient themselves with refined notions of old age homes and day care homes for the aged. In the name of parental affection, children should not be denied the opportunities to live and grow wherever they get a fertile land. Parents shouldn't be selfish to demand care from one's own children denying their future prospects; they have lived their lives and have achieved whatever they aspired for, now the time has come for the children to fulfill their aspirations. So why not let them off if that is their only choice. This doesn't mean that all children should take their parents to old age homes after extracting their money and services. If the situation is so demanding, we have to think about such an option where both parents and children would be equally relieved off tensions and helplessness. Phone calls, internet chatting and occasional get together and holidaying together will be fun and warmth for parents and children. In the case of bed ridden parents one must have the option to resort to the help of hospitals and home nurses. Even in such cases well equipped old age homes would be a better option for children who are far off struggling for a decent living.

Responsible home nursing care is an issue these days. Several instances of harassment by the home nurse and against the home nurse fill the columns of dailies. If it is properly professionalised and monitored appropriately, home nursing will be a blessing both for the jobless (less educated yet trained) men and women and nuclear families where both husband and wife are employed with nobody to take care of the aged.

Qn: In your opinion who should take the responsibility of looking after the parents if there is both a son and a daughter?

Ans: In the study conducted, one reason for son preference as suggested by the sample is that 'a son will look after the parents in their old age whereas the daughter will be married off to a different family'. Parents, whether, of the husband or the wife are parents to both. There should not be any discrimination in this regard among the couple. The son or daughter who is staying with the parents or employed nearest should willingly take the overall responsibility of parental care. But all children, both sons and daughters should share this responsibility. There are instances where the wife is not allowed to spend any of her earning for her parents. This is a cruel act that is to be discouraged at any cost. If the woman is earning, she must have the total control over her earning and the husband shouldn't interfere with how and where she spends it. Mutual sharing and consent, of course would ensure warmth and harmony in marital relationships provided there is no domination and submissiveness of any of the couples. When more and more daughters come forward to look after their parents, the son preference existing in the present society will start diminishing.

Qn: What solution would you recommend for improving women's power within the institution of marriage?

Ans: Proper socialisation of boys and girls from the very beginning whereby boys are also taught to respect the opposite sex, providing assertiveness training to girls, parental role models, economic independence of women, awareness generation regarding the need for gender equality among men and women are certain essential steps that would improve women's power within marriages.

Qn: In that case do employed wives have more power within marriage than their counterparts?

Ans: Definitely, research and experiences support more decision making power of wage earning wives.

Qn: But still there are a number of highly educated girls in our society who remain jobless in their search and waiting for the future husband. Why is it so?

Ans: There are plenty of highly educated girls who forget their identity in the search and waiting for husbands. This is because men and marriage are still overrated in the lives of women. Securing a husband and keeping him as one's own is very often considered as the goal of woman's life in several communities and families. The socialisation practices in families, media and religion instill a kind of 'Cindrella complex' in our girls which makes them wait for someone to come and act as their 'saviour'. Majority of school and college going girls are addicts of this complex and a girl may waste any amount of her time and energy to dream of the saviour and decorate herself while searching for the hero. The same complex is the culprit that makes the girl forget her identity.

Qn: Can you elaborate on the term 'identity'?

Ans: Women usually think of themselves and are known by others either as daughter, sister, wife or mother of someone, the someone very often being a man. With regard to men the case is different. In several instances women feel proud of and contended in being the mere echoes and shadows of men. Search for identity means discover one's self/ find out one's own space in the world - find true answers to questions like 'who am I, what am I capable of, what are my strengths and weaknesses, what is the purpose of my being' etc. The term 'one's own space' is a comprehensive one- including physical, intellectual, psychological and work space. A figural representation of the concept of 'one's own space' is given below:

A woman gets empowered only when she discovers her true identity. She must recognise the power within along with the weaknesses. It involves an internal transformation of one's consciousness which in turn is inevitable in enabling one to overcome the traditional ideologies and break the external barriers that are responsible for her oppression. A woman is said to have discovered her identity when she recognises her physical, intellectual, emotional and work spaces. Due to the improper socialisation they receive, girls face yet another question, whether they can have an identity of their own. Just as Erikson (1968) opined "our young girls very often ask whether they can have an identity of their own before knowing whom they are going to marry or for whom they are going to make a home". Our girls fail to discover their true self because of the

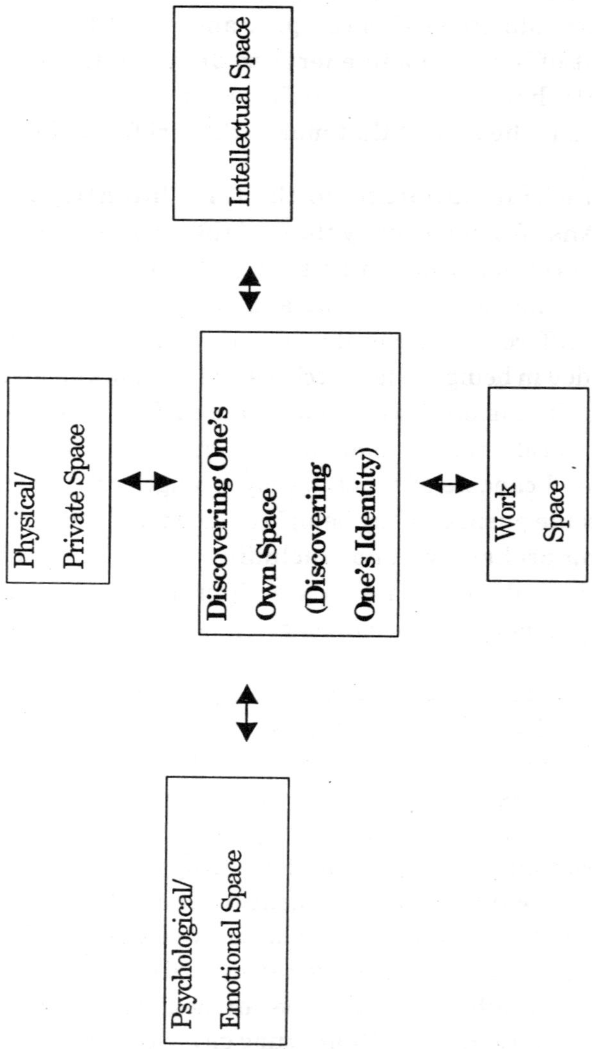
Intellectual Space
Physical/ Private Space
Discovering One's Own Space (Discovering One's Identity)
Work Space
Psychological/ Emotional Space

deeper internalisation of the patriarchal values and the subsequent development of a 'Hanuman Complex'- a feeling of worthlessness where one needs to be time and again reminded of the power within.

Qn: You speak about empowerment. What does it really mean? Why do we speak about women empowerment and not about men empowerment?

Ans: Women Empowerment as a concept was introduced at the third International Women's Conference at Nairobi in 1985. The Conference defined 'women empowerment as a redistribution of social power and control of resources in favor of women.' Control over resources in turn include control both over societal resources like education, employment and political power and house hold resources like income, property, health, nutrition and decision making. For gaining this control one must primarily have the access to these resources. In our country the discriminatory practices in the form of differential socialization of boys and girls very often deny this access to girls.

Women are the ones who are marginalised and treated as objects for men's pleasure, there is no respect for their souls and minds, their bodies are misused and thrown out, they are the last and least fed within the homes, they are the last to be hired and first to be fired in matters related to employment. The case for men is entirely different. **Do we need masters and slaves in families where women live a life of suspended animation? Do we need lions and deers in society where our daughters live a life of fear and terror?** No, what we need is peace and happiness in families and gender equality and justice in the society where our women live a happy life of partnership and companionship with men and our girls live a full, fearless, beautiful life with dignity just like boys. That is why women are to be empowered. It is jokingly said that if our men are empowered enough the question of women empowerment wouldn't arise at all.

Qn: Men generally seem to have a dislike for the emphasis given to women empowerment programmes. Why?

Ans: This dislike exists among a few due to lack of proper awareness. Empowerment is not a question of fight with men. Moreover, as opined by Amartya Sen women empowerment can positively influence the lives not only of women themselves but also of men and children. Gender inequality affects boys and men through biological connections and also through societal connections.

Qn: Who is an empowered woman?

Ans: Empowerment is self-sufficiency, self-governance and maintenance. From the stand point of UNESCO's gender empowerment index, a person becomes empowered when she is able to make decisions for herself and others, socially and politically. A woman becomes fully empowered only when she enables or facilitates another person to grow and develop. An Empowered woman will be having creative and liberating power channelised for the welfare of others (Power with) and not destructive power to control and dominate others (Power over).

Qn: What are the strategies to be adopted for ensuring empowerment of women individually and collectively?

Ans: Empowerment is not something that could be given or added into a woman from outside by an external agency. At the same time an external agency can facilitate the empowerment of a woman through appropriate interventions in the form of capacity building, consciousness raising, legal awareness generation, entrepreneurship training etc. Strategies for empowering women vary greatly and depend on the particular state of the women at the time of intervention. This could be better explained with the help of Longwe's (2002) Women's Empowerment Framework which identifies and defines the following five levels of empowerment:

(a) Welfare: which is defined as the lowest level, at which a development intervention may hope to close a gender gap and ensure the meeting of basic needs of women.

(b) Access: This is defined as the first level of empowerment, since women improve their own status, relative to men, by their own work and organization arising from increased access to resources such as education, employment, land and credit.

(c) Conscientisation: This is defined as the process by which women realize that their lack of status and welfare, relative to men, is not due to their own lack of ability, organization or effort but due to the discrimination against women. The urge to remove these discriminatory practices will also be developed at this stage.

(d) Mobilization: This means women's collective action to analyze and identify the discriminatory practices that stand in their way, and collective and strategic action to remove these discriminatory practices.

(e) Control: This is the level that is reached when women have taken action so that there is gender equality in decision making over access to resources whereby women have achieved direct control over their access to resources, and are no longer 'given' resources merely at the discretion of men, or by the whim of patriarchal authority (Longwe, 2002).

The strategy to be adopted for facilitating the empowerment of a school/ college student will be entirely different from that for a less educated, unemployed married woman. It is to be designed only after identifying the state / level of the individual woman / women's group that requires an intervention.

Qn: In spite of the accelerated women empowerment programmes going on in our country for the last few decades, the condition of women does not show any marked improvement. Why?

Ans: Empowering women as a process demands a life cycle approach. It has different dimensions at different levels as follows:

Psychological- better self image, courage and confidence

Economic - economic independence and self reliance

Social - awareness and access to all societal resources

Political - decision making for oneself and others

It is a long drawn conscious and continuous process comprising enhancement of skills, capacity building, gaining self confidence and meaningful participation in decision making. Hence empowerment basically needs a psychological process of transformation to reverse the feeling of learned helplessness among women leading to an increase in knowledge, capacity, self confidence and self reliance. Such an internal transformation of one's consciousness is inevitable in enabling one to overcome the traditional ideologies and break the external barriers to access to resources. This is lacking in our empowerment programmes. What we often do is an allopathic treatment of the symptoms of women's issues but what we should do is a homeopathic treatment of the actual cause for the problems. The actual cause often is the improper socialisation and the subsequent internalisation of the learned helplessness. The National Policy for Empowerment of Women, 2001 however adopts a holistic approach towards women empowerment.

Qn: Could you please elaborate on the National Policy for Empowerment of Women?

Ans: The National Policy for Empowerment of Women has specific goals and objectives laid down for the advancement, development and empowerment of women, the attainment of which would serve to enhance the dignity of girl children. The goals are listed below:

(i) Creating an environment through positive economic and social policies for full development of women to enable them to realize their full potential.

(ii) The *de-jure* and *de-facto* enjoyment of all human rights and fundamental freedom by women on equal basis with men in all spheres – political, economic, social, cultural and civil.

(iii) Equal access to participation and decision making of women in social, political and economic life of the nation.

(iv) Equal access to women to health care, quality education at all levels, career and vocational guidance, employment, equal remuneration, occupational health and safety, social security and public office etc.

(v) Strengthening legal systems aimed at elimination of all forms of discrimination against women.

(vi) Changing societal attitudes and community practices by active participation and involvement of both men and women.

(vii) Mainstreaming a gender perspective in the development process.

(viii) Elimination of discrimination and all forms of violence against women and the girl child; and

(ix) Building and strengthening partnerships with civil society, particularly women's organizations.

Qn: In shaping outlooks and attitudes of our youngsters, the influence of media seems more important than parental socialisation.

Ans: Exactly. Media plays such a prominent role in gender stereotyping that both print and electronic media serve as agents of patriarchy. The invisibility and inaudibility of women in society is perpetuated and enhanced by the print media while the visual media act as stronger institutions of patriarchy perpetuating the stereotypic images of women as housewives and mothers.

Qn: Could you elaborate on what is meant by gender stereotypism?

Ans: Gender stereotypes are preconceived notions about individuals based on their sex. The society arbitrarily believes and assigns certain personality traits, roles and behaviours to men and women. Breaking the stereotypes calls forth much opposition and alienation from the society and hence people rarely dare to do it. Gender stereotyping puts an unfair burden on girls and women placing them always at the looser's end. For example, men are considered as breadwinners while women are considered as housewives. Because of this stereotypic notion, parents invest more in the education of boys than that of girls. Pre and post market discriminations in employment opportunities have also their roots in this stereotypic notion.

Qn: How do print media lead to the devaluation of girls and women?

Ans: The activities of the wealthy and powerful are reported prominently while those of the poor and marginalized, including women are left out from the print. The absence of women from the news pages is what Gaye Tuchman terms 'symbolic annihilation' – a combination of condemnation, trivialization and erasure. Even though the press does not totally ignore women's issues, the coverage remains far from satisfactory. A glance through the women's pages of our newspapers and magazines including women's magazines reveal the undue weightage given to women's image as sex symbols, piece of décor or housewife. Fashion, decor and style fill the columns of dailies and pages of magazines. Of course one needs all these in the present glamour world and need not look on them skeptically. However the extreme significance attached to them develops an addiction among the young and old for the fancy world that they forget even the meaning and aim of life. The passion for the glamour world generates the need for huge money in its consumers. An analysis of the rape and sexual harassment cases that have filled the columns reveals how the craze for glamour and quick money has led to the trapping up of several youngsters in sex rackets.

Qn: Would you like to say that the print media is having a misguiding influence on youngsters?

Ans: Definitely, the success stories driven more by anatomy than talent are highlighted in the media. The adolescent girls find their role models among those who step in the ramp or sparkle in the video light. It is the responsibility of the print media to project role models who are brainy, creative and talented intellectuals and decision makers and who are sensitive to fellow women's needs and concerns, rather than focusing on achievements of beauty and glamour alone. Just as a writer argues, whose fault is it that dubious success stories of beauty queens are given more footage and column inches by the media than stories of real grit and courage? The media should recognize the hidden danger of shrinking a woman's mental horizon to the short lived passions and fantacies of the consumerist culture. Media should enable them to cut across the borders of age-old walls of inferiority imposed upon them, encourage them to think high and break the walls of silence nurtured among them and give them enough space to share their needs, feelings and thoughts. Real talent must be the judgment used for allocating space rather than beauty, political or religious affiliations.

Qn: But has not been media highly successful in bringing forth violence against women to the limelight?

Ans: The role played by media in bringing out violence against women to the limelight is quite significant. But while pursuing such a noble cause, the victims of violence especially that of sexual harassment are in a way mentally harassed by the media stories. As opined by a member of the State Women's Commission, the young girl passing through a condition of mental trauma due to sexual rape is further subjected to mental rape by the media. Media turns a blind eye towards the actual reasons of women's subordination and factors responsible for the sustenance of women's oppression. Instead of highlighting the severity of male promiscuity, gravity of the loopholes in the social security system and the lackadaisical approach adopted by the authorities, the media unleash an attack on the dress code or morality of the victimized. Working women approaching the complaints committee of Universities and other institutions very often express their fear of media harassment as a reason for their belated responses.

Qn: What is the role played by visual media in the devaluation of girls?

Ans: Women are often depicted as passive, dependent, lacking initiative and decision making power. There will not be a single episode in serials lacking a scene of women shedding tears. The growing girls learn hard to burst into tears at the slightest element of discomfort just as their ideal feminine character who is depicted in cinemas and serials as crying out easily where upon the man around –either friend, lover, husband or father starts loving and caring her all the more strongly. Even though bursting into tears is never a panacea for helplessness, the visual media often disseminates the message that to be silly and crying out is an ideal practice for an ideal girl who is to be tender, delicate and soft like a flower.

Women are also depicted as interested in showing off whereby they dress up to catch the attention of men and engage in tricky gestures to lure men. Dressing up which is to be conceived of as an aspect of one's personality and of course, as an element that contributes to confidence building and as an effort to make oneself presentable and acceptable, is misinterpreted as a purposeful act to provoke the opposite sex or to seduce them. Another degrading image of women projected in cinemas and serials is that of the mother in law who is cruel, wicked and fault finding. This in turn transmits two kinds of messages – the immediate message that there is nothing unusual in exerting control over daughter in law and an ultimate message that a woman's enemy is always yet another woman. Women are rarely shown in unconventional careers or in positions of power and authority. Even if we come across such a woman character, she is shown as inefficient and foolish but successfully continuing in the post due to the support of a saviour – 'the man' either in the role of a lover or a father who is competent, intelligent and powerful whereas the woman is devalued as a foolish, emotional and sexy creature.

Qn: Even high police officials make such observations that woman begets harassment because of her dressing style. How do you view this?

Ans: Such observations often made by police officers and political leaders hand over a license to the offenders to harass any girl who may appear attractive in her dressing. These statements also convey the message that attractive girls are all bad in character and if a girl/woman wants to protect herself she must look weird and ugly and in the name of modesty cover up her whole body in dresses so as to appear disgusting to the penetrating eyes. This can only add up to the feelings of inadequacy and helplessness in girls. Proper dressing is a matter that adds to the confidence of any human being. As said earlier decorating oneself as a technique of attention calling is to be discouraged in our school and college going students. But harassing the young ones and blaming the dressing style of girls is a serious issue that is to be condemned at any cost. Instead of punishing the offenders for their lack of self control, it has become a recent trend to justify them and even the educated and mature men folk join hands in suggesting for dress code for girls and working women. Is our morality so fragile that the media also supports such a bad notion without taking into consideration the atrocities directed against well dressed women, women in purdah and girls in school uniforms.

Qn: There is a current trend in visual media to portray women at either end of the two extremes and to depict smart girls as wicked and treacherous propagating wrong notions about smart and active girls.

Ans: This is very true. The traditional image of a full time housewife is glorified in cinemas and serials whereas the educated and career women are most often portrayed as arrogant, mavericks and home wreckers. There are serials in which co-sisters falling into either of these extremes are portrayed, depicting two extreme notions about womanhood. Of course cinema/serials being reproduction of real life, there is every chance to come across every type of character in a particular serial/cinema. But when these extreme portrayals take their 'avataars' in the same serial, in the same episode, its message to the young girls will be depressing. They help only to reinforce the gender stereotypes.

Qn: Is it true that cinemas and serials degrade women by perpetuating violence against women?

Ans: In almost all the movies and serials there will be acts of men beating up or ridiculing or directing other kinds of violence against women. This in turn makes younger boys to think that violence is an acceptable and effective way to solve conflicts and younger girls to conceive the wrong notion that men have the right to inflict pain on them. This is supported by the findings of the study, UNFPA (2005) on gender based violence conducted by the Sakhi Resource Centre for Women, Thiruvananthapuram that almost one third of the sample of 900 housewives, under study believed that a husband has the right to beat his wife. Also the grown up women who are dependent on their partners emotionally and economically learn to endure violence as part of being loyal to their husbands. Cinema and serials very often highlight the sanctity of such silent sufferers to the extent that silence of women on the face of violence is regarded as a symbol of nobility of the woman. A number of studies have concluded that viewing television violence increases aggressive behaviour in children and adolescents. (Sege and Dietz, 1994; Liebert and Sprafkin, 1998). Eron (1994) reported a significant correlation between the seriousness of crimes for which males were convicted by the age of 30 and their taste for violent programmes in Television at the age of 8.

Qn: Women activists often complain of objectification of women in the media. What is it and how does it contribute to degrading the dignity of women?

Ans: Objectification of womanhood is a frequent phenomenon in the visual media. Woman is depicted as an object for man's pleasure without giving any respect or consideration for her individuality, her feelings and desires. She is minimised into a mere body and commodity. There are several instances in which man own and disown woman as per his whims and moods and the deserted woman remain in learned hopefulness, hoping for the day when her lord returns to own her up. At other times woman is depicted as a goddess who is ready to forgive and forget the cruelties and damages done to her. If at all she is treated as a living thing she is given the status of a helpless creature who knows only to extend unconditional love and loyalty to her lover or husband. Women are most often portrayed as irrational beings who own a body that is emotional and erotic so as to please men and neither possessing a mind nor a soul. One is tempted to conclude that women are depicted in the visual media in a manner that pleases the patriarchal male gaze. Such portrayals serve only to strengthen the learned inferiority of women and learned superiority of the opposite sex. The pornographic media content are not only offensive and symbolically degrading but also might become stimulus to rape and violence of the 'pleasure giving object', the Woman !

Qn: Could you suggest some ways by which media can serve to enhance the dignity of girl children?

Ans: In a society where strong son preference and aversion to girl child exists, the media should share its responsibility in the emancipation of the subjugated gender by portraying positive images of girls and women. Visual media has a powerful potential to support women empowerment programmes going on in the country. The continued projection of negative and degrading images of women in movies and serials must be changed and they should provide a balanced picture of women's diverse lives and contributions to the society. Violence in the visual media at any cost should be minimized so that our youngsters no longer imitate it and become perpetuators of violence in their turn. Also offenders should be given strict punishment at least in the virtual world so that one could be tempted to think about such a possibility. Being a true depiction of social relationships and culture, whatever violence that occur in the society would find a place in serials and movies. But instead of picturising women as weak, fragile and giving up on the face of problematic situations, a refined image of womanhood as strong, bold and courageous, willing to take up challenges and aware of her rights should be portrayed.

Depicting healthy friendships between opposite sex should be encouraged in the visual media so that the young and old alike come to terms with the notion of friendship with the other sex which today is most often viewed through a distorted lens.

Portraying of young girls as falling easy victims to rich boys is to be avoided on various grounds. On the one hand it generates a fear among parents about the vulnerability of young girls and women who in turn curtail the mobility of girls. On the other hand such portrayals aggravate the hegemonic feelings of men to lay hands on women's bodies as a kind of birth right. Instead of highlighting the helplessness of poor girls, the serials should portray the will power and courage of girls to withstand such pressures.

Depiction of women as having extramarital affairs and pre-marriage pregnancies is quite common in our serials. This conveys a dangerous message that women are generally slaves to their sexual passions and have a weak morality. It is also a common feature in most of our cinema/serials that women quarrel with each other for a man just as dogs fight for a piece of bone. Such an overemphasizing of the role of man in a woman's life convey the obsolete message that marriage is the be-all and end-all for girls, which in turn would lead to early marriages and teenage pregnancies.

Career women in the visual media are often shown as torn between role conflicts which pass on a discouraging message to young girls in taking up jobs and becoming economically independent. In fact in such cases the media has a missionary role to play by promoting the equal sharing of family responsibilities by both husband and wife and depicting non-stereotypic gender roles of men and women within the family. This in turn may prove useful in eliminating spousal and child abuse and all forms of violence against women including domestic violence. While highlighting the glory of motherhood the media has to disseminate the message of equal parenting by both spouses. Today mothering, home making and caring for the old are all considered as sole responsibilities of women. Only media can come to the rescue of the sufferers. Pleasant home experience where the man is equally involved in cooking, washing, cleaning and other household chores is a message that the media should take up immediately without waiting for a second thought if it is to support gender justice.

Our girls need empowering examples of women achievers to inspire them as they live in a country where women are dwindling in numbers and abuse and discrimination are accepted as norms of civilization. More of women leaders and successful career women are to be portrayed on how they manage work and family responsibilities as mother, as professional and as entrepreneurs with or without spousal help so as to provide role models to the youngsters.

The media should always highlight and enhance the human rights of women in all spheres. Being the most widespread and influential medium, television particularly has to utilize its powerful potentials to create a civic sense in men and women to enhance the dignity of girl child.

Qn: Do you mean to say that the media should project positive images of women and negative images of men?

Ans: Images of strong women do not imply a negative or weak image of men. Men and women should be treated equally with gender justice. Just as there are weak and wicked men in the world, there should be weak and wicked women. What is needed is a breaking of gender stereotypes of both men and women and depiction of independent and efficient women in all spheres of life. Observational learning in turn may do wonders for our men and women.

In a patriarchal society, the media should support the subjugated gender by portraying how improper socialization would make girls economic liabilities and how proper socialization and timely investment in education would turn them out as assets to families. The visual media should lend a supportive hand to the contemporary women's movements to put an end to the devaluation of women in society.

Qn: Are girls and women equally productive as boys and men economically?

Ans: Why not? There are numerous women who excel men in their workplace. In several instances women are found to be more committed to work and less corrupted. At home, in the field and in the factories and offices, a closer observation would reveal that women work much more and much harder than men.

Qn: The Managers, Directors and Heads of offices are often men, not women. Why?

Ans: The posts you have mentioned are all managerial posts which require more leadership qualities. They are all prestigious and high paid jobs. A society like ours always allocates such higher jobs to men. Women very often will have to face lot of challenges at workplace including harassment from the male colleagues and subordinates if ever she dares to occupy such posts. The discrimination and cumulative backwardness that I mentioned earlier also play a part here.

Qn: Girls are found to fall easy preys of trafficking now a days. How can you prevent this?

Ans: Girls need help in the building up and maintenance of effective interpersonal relations with others. They must be enabled to safeguard their 'psychological space' from all disturbing elements which may turn out as stumbling blocks to personal growth. At the same time girls must be made aware of the need to fix boundaries and limit themselves in all their relations so as to avoid chances of exploitation. A sixth sense must be developed in our girls and women to enable them to sense danger in the form of unhealthy advances so as to avoid unpleasant consequences. Youngsters must be made aware of the impacts of materialism and hedonistic tendencies to which they are very likely to fall preys. A girl who is worried about the inability of her parents to meet high dowry demands when approached by a man with attractive promises of marriage without dowry, naturally will fall easy prey for all his fantacies. Girls must be made aware of their worthiness and encouraged to ignore such false promises. Love and respect for one's body must be nurtured as a value in girls and boys. Severe punishment of offenders must be ensured to prevent unhealthy practices. We should also put an end to the portrayal of woman as a sex object by the media.

Qn: Your suggestions to stop the dowry system?

Ans: Yes, that is what we have been discussing all this time. Make the girls economically productive in an equal manner as the boys and enhance their dignity. Ensure equal inheritance rights for both sons and daughters. Awareness to the public regarding how the dowry system is detrimental to the very existence of girls on this earth is to be provided through massive campaigning. Special appreciation and incentives to be given to couples who have entered the wedlock without dowry. Components on gender sensitisation and violence against women, including dowry system are to be ensured in the school and college curriculum. The youth, especially boys should come forward to marry without taking any dowry and the girls should make it a point not to marry boys who ask for dowry. The local self governments should take a proactive role to put an end to this social evil. A typical example in this regard is provided by the Nilambur Grama Panchayat in Malappuram district of Kerala. The panchayat fed up with the grievances of thousands of girls wedded through 'Mysore Kalyanam', a type of interstate marriage system, specially prevalent in Nilambur area, has taken the initiative to nip the evil from the bud. Strict implementation of the Dowry Prohibition Act with community participation is yet another measure that can prevent the dowry menace.

Qn: What is the influence of globalisation on the dignity of girls and women?

Ans: What globalisation offers to the world is a mix of blessings and curses, pluses and minuses. It has dramatically changed the lives of both men and women in all spheres of life over the world. Rapid social changes, consumerist culture, stiffer competitions, disruption of families, increasing violence, loss of tolerance, increased individualism and selfishness are features of the present globalised society. The impact of globalisation on women needs to be assessed in the light of women's multiple roles as productive and reproductive labour in their families as well as their contributions towards overall community cohesion and welfare, and maintaining the social fabric. Globalisation offers both blessings and cursings to women all over the world.

Qn: What are the blessings of globalisation to women?

Ans: Increase in literacy and educational standards along with benefits of family planning, health care, child care and job opportunities have served in boosting up the self confidence of women. The IT enabled jobs in call centres, BPOs and medical transcription recruit young women in large numbers who so far used to remain jobless and hopeless. Increased access to micro-credit, employment opportunities and information for women in poorer sections due to ICT is yet another contribution of globalisation. The mass production of labour saving devices like cookers, washing machines, microwave ovens etc. have served a lot in reducing the drudgery of women in their housewife roles.

Qn: How far have these changes contributed to enhancing the dignity of women?

Ans: Increase in job opportunities has raised the self confidence and sense of independence among girls and women. By bringing them into workforce, globalisation has given women the power to question the system that breeds poverty, exploitation and oppression. The economically poor and socially exploited image of traditional women has changed drastically, with more egalitarian set of gender relations at least in urban areas. More opportunities for migration and exposure at international level have widened the mental and physical horizons of women. Globalisation has given women a new identity, financial independence, freedom of expression as well as a remarkable social status. At the same time globalization has pressurized women by putting a double burden of maintaining a balance between home and work front. Whether globalization has truly helped women in their struggle for identity and equal status as human beings or has it only changed the manner of age-old exploitation putting more burden and pressures is a topic of serious discussion.

Qn: What are the negative impacts of globalisation on women?

Ans: Even though globalisation has led to increasing job opportunities for women, most of them are employed in the unorganized sector very often in contractual employment that are irregular and unstable. Those women in export processing zones work in poorly paid, mentally and physically unhealthy and insecure situations The domestic responsibility of women still remains unchanged whereby several of them suffer a lot of role conflicts. Privatization of education and health sectors has the worst impacts on women. It has become more difficult for women to get higher education especially professional education in Indian families. Loss of resources, traditional skills and knowledge of women along with Increasing number of Female Headed Households have led to the emergence of new phenomena like feminization of poverty and feminization of employment. Curtailment of state provisions in child care, community care and social security has increased the dual burden of women. All over the world girls from poor countries are recruited in rich countries as domestic labour. International exploitation and trafficking of women are on the rise. Another important impact is the identity confusion created by globalization that gets reflected in issues like depression, suicide, alcoholism and substance abuse. The increased materialistic greed among youngsters in turn has resulted in a hike in dowry rates, prostitution, abuse and dowry related suicides.

Qn: How far have these changes contributed to lowering the dignity of girls and women?

Ans: Increase in sex tourism in most parts of third world countries as a form of bringing foreign exchange and making the country an appealing vacation destination has reduced women into mere bodies and commodities for men's pleasure. In the new consumerist culture, their bodies are misused and thrown out. Objectification of women's bodies in advertisements and rising atrocities against women have also lowered the dignity of girls. Increase in dowry demands, teenage pregnancies and abortions and increase in suicide rates are all evidences to the lowered dignity of girls in the globalised society.

Qn: How can we prevent the negative impacts of globalisation?

Ans: Globalization is irresistible and irreversible. In spite of advancement in some aspects, gender inequality continues to be all pervading. Because of deep rooted differences in gender roles and socio-cultural expectations, the impact of globalization is felt differently by men and women and by women belonging to different class, race and culture. The only choice before us is to think globally and act locally. Consumerist culture, high cost of living, high cost of education, increasing violence and lack of safety, increasing dowry demands, commodification of women's bodies, sex tourism, misuse of mobiles and internet, denigrating women's image in the media, over medicalisation of women's bodies, depletion of environmental resources, the list goes endless are the new challenges for the emancipation of women in the global world.

The remedy to reduce the negative aspects of globalisation lies in a combined and organised resistance to it by the government and the governed. Governments have to chalk out programmes and policies to safeguard the interests of the sufferers. Youngsters must be made aware of the impacts of the consumerist culture, materialism and hedonistic tendencies to which they are very likely to fall preys. The extreme pleasure seeking principle must be discouraged at any cost to ensure social health. Love and respect for one's body must be nurtured as a value in youngsters. The significance of moral and spiritual values for a peaceful life must be emphasized.

Qn: Would you suggest any special programmes for girls and women?

Ans: Capacity building and proper sensitisation of girls and women to resist the evils is highly essential. Correct knowledge and proper attitudes towards sexuality are to be developed in our girls. Girls need help in the building up and maintenance of effective interpersonal relations with family members, peers, teachers and all elders. They must be made aware of the need to fix boundaries and limit themselves in all their relations so as to avoid chances of exploitation. An analysis of the rape and sexual harassment cases that have filled the columns of dailies reveals how the craze for glamour and quick money has led to the trapping up of several youngsters in sex rackets. Girls must also be helped to select appropriate role models so as to facilitate their emancipation. Awareness regarding the use and misuse of technological advancements like mobiles and internet must be given to all girls. Instances of atrocities against women at home, workplace, roads etc. which are reported in newspaper and television should be made use for active discussion in women's groups with a view to develop timely alternative ways and means of self help in them at the face of problematic situations.

There are good number of laws and provisions for safety and security of girls and women in the society. But the socialization process teaches the girls not to respond but to adjust and suffer in silence all unwelcome advances and atrocities directed against them. Along with assertiveness training they must be made aware of their legal rights and the way to make use of the legal provisions for their safety. Media literacy, mobile literacy and legal literacy have become essential requisites for a woman to live in the globalised society to protect her basic human rights.

Qn: Could you elaborate on media literacy and mobile literacy?

Ans: Several researches support the finding that, depictions whether good or bad, cruel or soft in the television can strongly influence the human mind which has a natural tendency to imitate whatever it is exposed to, especially in the magic box. Psychological theories of observational learning, emotional contagion and conditioning explain the process by which violence, negative portrayal and degrading images of women depicted in the visual media can have vulnerable impacts in shaping up the outlooks, attitudes and behaviours of men and women where women always are at the loser side. In this instance what is needed is developing awareness among men and women that whatever is depicted in the media need not be always true and real and hence should not be internalised and imitated as such. Instead they should be enabled to make a selective internalisation of the real and rejection of the unrealistic fantacies. Media literacy also includes the awareness for not being misguided by the representations given in the media and making a judicious and logical screening between what is acceptable and what is not acceptable.

Now a days mobile has become a part and parcel of every individual, young and old, rich and poor, literate and illiterate, men and women. If judiciously used its merits outweigh its demerits to a great extent. But a lot of problems are emerging because of the misuse of mobiles by immature hands, with a heavy toll on women's privacy and security. Mobile literacy does not mean learning the skills to operate the mobile phones but learning to use the service of mobile phone facilities judiciously. Our girls must be taught to use it in a mature way, not being subjected to harassment and victimisation by the unsocial elements which sometimes may include their close friends, fellow passengers, classmates or relatives. They should be taught how to ignore unwanted messages and phone calls and how to deal with instances of cyber crime and pornography.

Qn: What is the role of education in enhancing the dignity of girls?

Ans: Education has always been considered as the most powerful instrument for bringing about attitudinal changes and social change. It was in this respect that the National Policy of Education, 1986 viewed education to play a positive interventionist role in the empowerment of women. Education is the only means to arouse social consciousness and bring about a change in the traditional patriarchal mindsets of men and women. Only proper education can instill the knowledge, capacities and skills in women that would equip them with the coping strategies inevitable to cut one's safe path amidst violence and atrocities and to lead a successful life in the modern society.

Education enables a woman to become economically independent through viable employment, education gives woman a sense of accomplishment and enhances her self confidence and self esteem, it enables her to understand the social structure and forces of oppression in a better way and react to them in a responsible manner. Education also empowers a woman to take informed choices and decisions. Thus the contribution of education to enhancing the dignity of girls and women is so comprehensive and extensive.

Qn: But there are several educated women in our society who fail to face the challenges of life and live a life of worthlessness and hopelessness

Ans: Yes, the present system of education has only served to worsen the condition of women. It has served a lot to improve their educational qualifications without contributing much to improve their actual conditions. I have come across a girl who was a first rank holder for her post graduation but committed suicide immediately afterwards before even getting her degree certificate. Girls who used to excel in their studies have turned out to be utter failures in real life. All these pinpoint certain lacunae in our educational system. The undue preference for quantitative mass education to quality promotion and breakaway from essential holistic education to serve the needs of technology and business rather than a balanced transition is doing more harm than good. The affective domain seems to be totally neglected by the educationists. Today the Indian higher education system is strengthening its pursuit for meeting technological needs of the modern world at par with international standards. The thrust on Engineering, Management Studies and IT is essential to equip our youth to meet global needs. But this must not deny the need for components on social justice and peaceful living. Our education system fails on one side to enable the girls to discover their identity and on the other side to enable boys to respect the individuality of girls. Now what is required is a curricular intervention that would equip our girls and women with the coping strategies against violence and discrimination and make our boys gender sensitised. It may take the form of an awareness programme for the illiterate and grown-up men and women who are out of the educational system whereas it can be in the form of curricular components for those within the system.

Qn: Can you suggest examples for such curricular components?

Ans: The adolescence education programme at the secondary and higher secondary school levels, the NSS programmes at college levels, the community living camp in colleges of teacher education, the life skill education programme in colleges, gender sensitisation programmes in colleges and universities are all aimed at developing social awareness, social commitment and special skills and capacities in youngsters to face violence and discrimination and not to become perpetrators of such evils.

Qn: Could you please elaborate on the components of a life skill education programme for girls?

Ans: The life skill education is based on the principle of human rights that every girl has an equal right to live a life of dignity on this planet. The outline of a life skill education programme designed and practiced by the author for girls at under graduate and post graduate levels is given below:

Life Skill Education - An Outline

• Personality Development	Catering to development of self esteem, self confidence, balanced personality; Leadership and Capacity building; Acquaintance with IT world etc.

(Contd.)

(Contd. Table)

• Stress Management	Dealing with stressors of all types, Stress reduction techniques, Time management; Practice of Yoga and Meditation etc.
• Health and Sexuality	Dealing with Physical, Mental; Spiritual and Social health; Reproductive health and Sexuality; HIV/AIDS etc.
• Social Relations	Building and maintenance of inter-personal relations; Communication and social skills etc.
• Value Education	Moral and Spiritual values; Impacts of Materialism and Hedonism; Significance of values in life; Respect for opposite sex; Responsible behavior to the poor, disabled and marginalized etc.
• Human Rights	Human rights of different groups and sections in the society; Women's rights as human rights; Responsibility for protecting human rights etc.
• Social Awarness	Current issues and problems in the society; Corruption and violence; Communal disharmony; Atrocities against women, children and marginalized sections; Nuclearisation of world; Protection of environment; Responsibilities of Youth etc.

Qn: What is the role of schools and colleges in propagating patriarchal values and perpetuating gender stereotypes?

Ans: Our educational institutions often serve as pillars of patriarchy. The teachers and educational administrators who are products of patriarchy are totally unaware of the need for gender equality and they happen to act as agents spreading patriarchal values. For example, boys are encouraged to take up leadership roles both in schools and colleges and girls however smart they may be will have to satisfy with the posts of assistant school leader in schools and vice chairperson and joint secretary roles in colleges and universities. The wise girls will have to satisfy with the vice/ assistant roles whereas the boys just being boys will be offered the superior posts and roles. What a tragedy! When you organise a programme at such institutions, boys sit on the dais while girls will be put in charge of reception and decorating the hall, the boy will make the welcome speech while the girls will offer the bouquet to the guests, the boys will discuss the matters with the guests while the girls will serve the food to the guests. Directly and indirectly such practices strengthen the stereotypic roles in girls and boys.

As part of co curricular activities like SUPW, boys will get training in repair of electrical appliances while girls will be taught stitching and embroidery. In schools girls will be asked to sweep the floor and clean the classroom while boys will be sent out to play. Yet another way of gender stereotyping! When it comes to textbooks, there are several instances of gender bias in all subjects, which recently are getting eliminated due to the pressures made by women activists.

Qn: Your suggestions for changing the situation?

Ans: Being brought up in a patriarchal world and having internalised the patriarchal values so deeply, the teachers and educational administrators unknowingly perpetuate gender stereotypism and propagate patriarchal values. As a corrective measure, teachers at all levels in schools and colleges should be given gender sensitisation training; once they become aware of the discrimination and damage they had been inflicting in the growing minds , they will change and become advocates of gender equality.

Qn: Do you think that religion can extend a helping hand to enhance the dignity of women?

Ans: Definitely, religion has a significant role to play here. Almost all religions consider men as superior and women as inferior, impure and sinful. Religious dogmas are misinterpreted by the religious leaders and practitioners who are all men so as to keep women secondary. Priesthood most often is accorded to men only. As per religious discourses, God, the creator is fully aware of the physiology like monthly periods of his own creation, the woman. Then how can one discriminate woman as impure based on her bodily functions? If the bodily functions and secretions related to men's body are acceptable to God and do not interfere with his performing religious rituals, they naturally shouldn't be considered as a barrier to women also. **When God does not discriminate between his creations (male and female), why should the creations themselves should venture into discriminating the fellow creations.** This is a kind of blindness that requires immediate treatment in the form of open intellectual discussions in groups and personal logical analysis by every human mind. Correct awareness and true interpretation of the holy books in every religion should be promoted. Such texts should be subjected to serious studies which in turn would remove the blindness of millions of religious fundamentalists and practitioners.

The personal and family laws, relating to marriage, divorce, inheritance, succession, adoption and guardianship have been guided by religious beliefs of respective communities. The sad part of these laws is the fact that most of these are anti women and women are being victimised by the recent trends of religious fundamentalism. Any law which comes in the way of women empowerment should be changed. Since religion has a deep and powerful influence on human minds, it should be utilised for curbing the sinful practices of gender discrimination, son preference and female foeticide. Religious leaders should rise upto the need of the time and promote women's active participation in public sphere so as to enhance the dignity of womanhood.

Qn: How far would the Uniform Civil Code, be a panacea for stopping the discrimination against women in certain communities?

Ans: The Uniform Civil Code that claims for equal rights for men and women in all matters relating to marriage, divorce, guardianship and custody of children remains as a distant reality because of the strong opposition by certain religious communities. The enactment of UCC is feared to interfere with the fundamental right to freedom of religion. In all personal laws there are differential standards for men and women with regard to marriage, divorce and property rights which is to be viewed as a shame to civilization. So in order to ensure gender justice, the first and foremost thing to be implemented is the enactment of the UCC. Those religious leaders who are capable of logical reasoning and progressive thinking should take the lead in this effort. This would add momentum to the process of enhancing the dignity of women from the status of a second sex.

Qn: What about the property rights of women? Will it help in enhancing the dignity of girls and women?

Ans: We have effective laws that ensure property rights of women. But such laws remain only in paper. When it comes to implementation, girls and women are denied of their due share. Brothers make use of social sanctions and violence to seize the landed property and other material assets from sisters even when both brothers and sisters have equal rights in the property of parents. In certain communities sisters get only half of the share of brothers from their parental property and when there are no sons to inherit, instead of the entire property going to the daughters, one part goes to the father's family members other than the wife and daughters. The UN statistics highlight this cruel situation of discrimination in property rights as follows:

"Women do more than 60% of the hours of work done in the world, but they get 10% of the world's income and own 1% of the world's property". Women constituting fifty percent of human population are to own fifty percent of world's property but are discriminated so strongly by men who are their husbands, brothers and other relatives that they barely have any property in their name and custody. The law enforcement officers and judiciary remain silent of this injustice; the human rights activists also keep silence on the face of this discrimination. Even when girls inherit family property they are converted into husband's share at the time or within a few months after marriage. Joint possession and ownership of property by husband and wife is something that remains as a dream even for the educated Keralite women. This cannot be attributed to the lack of awareness of men folk; it is only a means of dominating and ensuring power over women. Several studies have shown that when women do have tangible economic assets in their names, they are less susceptible to domestic violence than their counterparts. Experiences from the state of Delhi has revealed an increasing trend in registering landed properties in the names of women when the state declared a reduction in registration charges in the case of women owners. It is high time all states think in tune with Delhi example of Property Registration and stick to strict implementation of the protective legislative measures. Is the lack of economic assets a major reason responsible for the high incidence of domestic violence in Keralite homes is a topic that is to be studied in detail.

Qn: It sounds contradictory that educated women of Kerala are victims of domestic violence?

Ans: As has been opined by a police officer in one of the gender sensitisation classes on Domestic Violence Act 2005, 'if the domestic violence in Kerala homes is assessed on the grounds mentioned as per the definition given by the Act, it will be very difficult to identify any single home where there is no domestic violence'. The study conducted by the Washington based ICRW (2000) revealed that physical violence is prevalent in 64 percent households in urban non-slum sites in the Kerala capital with 62 percent households reporting psychological violence. In rural areas, incidence of physical violence was reported to be as high as 71 percent and psychological violence 69 percent. As per the study on gender based violence in Kerala commissioned by the UNFPA and conducted by the Sakhi Resource Centre for Women, Thiruvananthapuram, about 40 percent of the 900 housewives interviewed admitted that they were victims of domestic violence unleashed by their husbands and a sizeable number of them were injured badly enough to be rushed to the causality wing in hospitals. All forms of domestic violence exist in the Kerala society irrespective of caste, religion, educational status and economic background. Studies have revealed that the higher educational standards of Keralite women have only served to provoke the patriarchal male chauvinism use its muscle power to win over the intellectual and emotional powers of womanhood. The years of silence on the face of violence and the learned hopefulness of women have not improved but worsened their conditions. Wife beating that formerly existed in slums and lower working class families is gradually creeping into the middle class and rich families.

Qn: What is the reason for this rising trend in domestic violence?

Ans: Domestic violence in Kerala has its roots in a clutch of factors including power relations within the family, economic dependence of women, extreme materialistic outlook and pleasure seeking, alcoholism, personality disorders, negative portrayal of women's image in media and absence of adequate social support systems As per the UNFPA commissioned study in Kerala, alcoholism, suspicion, financial worries and dowry related quarrels were found to be the major reasons for family violence. Violence against women has been the heinous wand of patriarchy employed to exercise strict control over women. The patriarchal approach and attitude "Wife is always to be beaten" emotionally supports perpetrators to repeat the crime and the abused to put up with the abuse and learn ways of dealing to cope with it. This is supported by the findings of the study on gender based violence conducted by the Sakhi Resource Centre, Thiruvananthapuram that almost one third of the sample (900 housewives) believed that a husband has the right to beat his wife. All governmental and civil efforts to prevent violence remain unfruitful because of the patriarchal power relations existing in the society, which teach silence and helplessness to our girls as part of socialisation. So long as manliness is equated with muscle power and the ability to keep women in subjugation, violence is here to stay.

Qn: What is the role of law and judiciary in protecting the safety and dignity of girls and women?

Ans: The second major reason attributed for son preference in the study was 'the lack of security of girls in the society'. We have stringent laws to protect women from all types of atrocities. But at the level of implementation, loopholes will be digged out in each and every law, whereby the culprit comes out afresh for the next crime. As per the newly enacted Domestic Violence Act 2005, all sorts of violence at home from male members including, father, brothers, husband, in-laws and relatives are punishable. Even abuse of any nature is a crime. However, the loop holes in the laws let the perpetrators go scot free to return to continue where they left off. So the existing laws are to be made fool proof without any chance for mishandling them.

Strict punishment of the offenders without any chance of mercy and humanitarian consideration if implemented will serve a lot in curbing the rising atrocities against women. The police should be made more women friendly as women are reluctant to register complaints at police stations out of fear of the police. A victim is scared to death to approach a police station to lodge a complaint for fear being subjected to present the horrid details most of the times. The perversion of a few who indulge in this while humiliating the traumatized victim brings shame to the force and the country alike. In recent days there have been several reports where police happen to encourage girls and women to adjust and put up with the culprit or withdraw the complaint they have made. Women police personnel often do complain about the superiority attitude maintained by men colleagues. This happens due to the lack of gender sensitivity of the police personnel. They must be made aware of the conditions in which a woman dares to approach police – women's reactions on the face of violence - first denial, next minimising, the third stage of justifying and the final stage of adjusting and accommodating with the violence directed against her. Only when she fails in all these attempts a woman comes forward to the police to register a complaint. Hence gender sensitisation of all police personnel, both men and women must be ensured to promote the proper enforcement of laws.

Parents discourage girls from going for higher education and employment in distant places because of their fears regarding the safety of girls. Safe accommodation facilities for working women are to be ensured in all district headquarters and the responsibility of providing such facilities for girl students should be entrusted with the educational institutions themselves and as a package along with the employment in the case of government undertakings and offices. The prepaid cab facility is to be implemented in all transport stations including road, rail and air travel. In a train the moment a girl ask a stranger about the details of a station, she is marked as an easy prey. Hence yet another facility to be implemented on a war footing is the compulsory announcement or display of upcoming stations in railway compartments.

The 24 hours helpline services for women in distress that have started functioning in all districts of Kerala and almost all the major cities in other states, where immediate help is rendered to women in trouble, is a welcome move. On dialing a toll free number, the alert women police equipped with vehicles allocated for the sole purpose would reach the aggrieved at the earliest.

But along with a potent law, there should be effective conscientising of women to enable them break the walls of learned helplessness and learned hopefulness. Collective action of academicians, activists and NGO's is needed to develop the notion of "NO MORE SILENCE ABOUT VIOLENCE" in our women.

Conclusion

Today women are trying hard to shed their shells of passivity, dependence and helplessness. They want to be treated as capable, intelligent and active participants and contributors to the process of development on an equal footing with men. Modern women are not satisfied with their traditional roles as housewives and mothers alone. Just as men consider husband hood and fatherhood as secondary roles, our young women are on their pursuit to discover their true identity whereby wifehood and motherhood become secondary preferences. The young girls want to tear off the mask of nobility carried on by their elders whereby the ideal woman keeps a smile on the face in spite of her suffering in silence to ensure the integrity of the family. Young girls question the popular notion that men can do wrong just because men are men and women have to keep on their chastity and bear the responsibility of safeguarding the chastity of men.

Modern women have proved their efficiency in the economic, social and political spheres of life. She hates to be shy and fearful; she wants to be treated as human, neither as a second sex nor as a silent sufferer. She wants to lead a happy and complete life on this beautiful earth keeping her head high. Of course, these are all images applicable to an empowered woman – one who is confident and active, economically independent, socially committed and politically conscious, one who knows how to proceed on her path safely amidst the penetrating eyes and atrocities directed at her, one who is able to take decisions on her own and to be the agent of her own destiny.

The world has changed, culture has changed, lifestyles have changed, the notions of development and happiness have changed but the cultural image of woman only remains unchanged over the past 20 years. Majority of men and women still now would like to view woman as the traditional home bound housewife and mother, the irrational, stupid yet beautiful homemaker-in the care taker, nurturing, at service and pleasure giving roles. The various agencies of socialisation such as family, media, religion etc. conforms to the norms of the majority, skillfully forgetting its responsibility towards gender justice and gender equality. The age-old cultural image of womanhood is to be refined with the changing times so as to ensure better social health, peace and harmony via emancipation of the critical mass. Nothing can help a woman unless she is ready to help herself and for this, what is mostly needed is a psychological empowerment of the woman concerned through proper awareness of herself and the world around. Let us all strive to make a change in our own lives and help others to lead a beautiful life on this beautiful earth. Along with Vanitha, let us all sing together, the song of hope, assurance and commitment for the cause of fellow women:

"We shall overcome, We shall overcome,

We shall overcome, Some day

O, Deep in my heart, I do believe

That we shall overcome some day."

APPENDIX 1
Age-wise Data of Kerala Population – 2001

Age Group	*Total*	*Male*	*Female*
All ages	31841374	15468614	16372760
0-4	2765164	1409487	1355677
5-9	2544181	1295679	1248502
10-14	2987200	1523842	1463358
15-19	2984506	1484586	1499920
20-24	2983990	1440467	1543523
25-29	2786195	1296905	1489290
30-34	2516463	1185807	1330656
35-39	2466354	1154778	1311576
40-44	1951284	960397	990887
45-49	1926144	952021	974123
50-54	1437520	724701	712819

(Contd.)

(Contd. Appendix - I)

Age Group	*Total*	*Male*	*Female*
55-59	1130244	541668	588576
60-64	1032136	480345	551791
65-69	902015	399671	502344
70-74	613422	273293	340129
75-79	399089	173558	225531
80+	389013	157345	231668
Age not stated	26454	14064	12390

Source : Directorate of Census Operations, Kerala, 2001.

APPENDIX II

Sex Ratio in Various Districts of Kerala

District	*Population*			*0-6 Population*		
	P	*M*	*F*	*P*	*M*	*F*
Kasaragod	1204078	588083	615995	159002	81145	77857
Kannur	2408956	1152817	1256139	279803	142625	137178
Wayanad	780619	391273	389346	104058	53116	50942
Kozhikode	2879131	1399358	1479773	347146	177208	169938
Malappuram	3625471	1754576	1870895	551525	281449	270076
Palakkad	2617482	1266985	1350497	318884	162406	156478
Thrissur	2974232	1422052	1552180	332459	169777	162682
Ernakulam	3105798	1538397	1567401	338924	173413	165511
Idukki	1129221	566682	562539	134177	68155	66022

(Contd.)

(Contd. Appendix - II)

District	Population			0-6 Population		
	P	M	F	P	M	F
Kottayam	1953646	964926	988720	212622	108358	104264
Alappuzha	2109160	1014529	1094631	226408	115752	110656
Pathanamthitta	1234016	589398	644618	127024	64568	62456
Kollam	2585208	1249621	1335587	292599	149255	143344
Trivandrum	3234356	1569917	1664439	368515	187800	180715
Kerala	31841374	15468614	16372760	3793146	1935027	1858119

Source: Directorate of Census Operations, Kerala, 2001.

APPENDIX III
S P I

Directions : This inventory is proposed to study whether son preference exists in our society along with exploring the reasons for the same. Kindly co-operate with the present study by marking your valuable responses.

Tick the appropriate column.

Section A

1. Male ☐ Famale ☐

2. Educational Qualification

Upto Std. X ☐ Upto Degree ☐
Upto Postgraduation ☐ Professional Degree ☐

2. Monthly Income of Family

Upto 5000 ☐ 5001-15000 ☐ Above 15000 ☐

3. Religion

Christian ☐ Hindu ☐ Muslim ☐

Section B

1. Do you feel that son preference exists in Kerala society?
   Yes ☐ No ☐

2 Do you feel that female foeticide occurs in Kerala
   Yes ☐ No ☐

3. What is your personal opinion about female foeticide?
   (a) It is to be condemned . ☐
   (b) It may be permitted if the situation demands ☐
   (c) There is nothing wrong with it ☐
   Given below are ten beliefs which are popularly viewed as plausible reasons for son preference. Rank them in the order of 1,2,3 ....10 with rank 1 for the most prominent and rank 10 for the least prominent reason. For example : If you find 'Lack of security experienced by girl child' as the most prominent reason for son preference of the society, put **'1'** in the column against statement **'c'**. If the belief 'A son is essential to perform the funeral ceremonies' is the least significant reason put **'10'** in the column against statement **'g'**.

a	Economic burden necessitated by dowry to the girl	
b	Birth of son would add to the social status of the family	
c	Lack of security experienced by girl child	
d	A son would carry over the family lineage	
e	A girl is meant for another family	
f	A boy would bring financial gains to the family	
g	A son is essential to perform the funeral ceremonies	
h	A girl's life is full of miseries when compared to that of a boy	
i	A daughter brings disgrace to the family if she fails to get a suitable alliance	
j	A son will take care of parents during their old age	

Bibliography

BOOKS & JOURNALS

Agnihotri, S.B. (2003). Survival of the girl child: Tunneling out of the chakravyuha. Economic and Political Weekly, October 11.

Aravamudan Gita (2007). Disappearing daughters – The tragedy of female foeticide. India: Penguin Books.

Arnold, F. et al. (1998). Son preference, the family building process and child mortality in India. Population Studies, 52.

Arokiasamy, P. (2002). Gender preference, contraceptive use and fertility in India: Regional and development influences. International Journal of Population Geography, 8.

Athreya Venkatesh (2001). Census 2001: The Tamil Nadu picture. Frontline, 18 (9), Apr. 28- May 11.

Balasubramanian (2007). In Gupta.J.A.(Ed.), New reproductive technologies, women's health and autonomy – Freedom or dependency? New Delhi : Sage Publications.

Balse Maya (1982). The Indian female attitude towards sex. New Delhi: Chetana Publications.

Bhasin Kamla (2005). Understanding Gender. New Delhi : Women Unlimited.

Best, J.W. & Kahn, J.V. (2005). Research in education. New Delhi: Prentice Hall of India.

Bracken Hillary & Nidadavolu Vijaya (2005). Mixed messages? An analysis of communication materials on abortion and sex determination in Rajasthan. Economic and Political Weekly, August 27.

Bumiller Elisabeth (1994). May you be the mother of a hundred sons: A journey among the women of India. New York: Random House.

Chunkath. S.R. & Athreya.V.B. (1997). Female infanticide in Tamil Nadu: Some evidence. Economic and Political Weekly, April.

Dagar Rainuka (Ed.). (1998). Manual on women's development and gender justice. Chandigarh :Institute for Development and Communication.

Dharma Kumar (1983). Male utopias or nightmares? Economic and Political Weekly, January.

George Sabu et al. (1998). Female infanticide in rural south India. Search Bulletin, July-September, 12(3), 18-26.

George Sabu (2000). Female foeticide in India. Health Action, September.

Goodkind, D. (1996). On substituting sex preference strategies in East Asia: Does pre- natal discrimination? Population and Development Review, 22 (1), 111-25.

Gupta, S.C. & Kapoor, V.K. (2003). Fundamentals of mathematical statistics. New Delhi: Sultan Chand & Sons.

Gurung Madhu (2002). Demographic danger signals. Frontline, 17(2), Jan . 22 – Feb 04.

Jain, S.C. (1985). Women and technology. Jaipur: Rawat Publications.

Kuruvilla Moly & Aanand Layana (2009). An Investigation Into the Power Relations Between Husband and Wife Within Marriages.Osmania Journal of Women's Studies, Vol. II, March, 18-25.

Kusum (1993). The use of pre-natal diagnostic techniques for sex selection: The Indian scene. Bioethics, 7, 149-165.

Lingam Lakshmi (1990). New reproductive technologies in India: A print media analysis. Reproductive and Genetic Engineering: International Feminist Analysis, 3(1).

Lingam Lakshmi (Ed.). (1998). Sex detection tests and female foeticide: Discrimination before birth. In understanding women's health issues: A reader. New Delhi: Kali for Women.

Macklin Ruth (1995). The ethics of sex selection. Indian Journal of Medical Ethics, 3 (4), October-December.

Miller, B.D. (1981). The endangered sex: Neglect of female children in rural north India, Ithaca: Cornel University Press.

Moen Elizabeth (1991). Sex selective eugenic abortion: Prospects in China and India. Issues in Reproductive and Genetic Engineering. ISSN: 0958-6415.

Muthulakshmi, R. (1997). Female Infanticide: 115 Census and Solutions, New Delhi: Discovery Publishing House.

Patel Vibhuti (1984). Amniocentesis and female foeticide: Misuse of medical technology. Socialist Health Review, 1(2).

Patel Vibhuti (1989). Sex–determination and sex preselection tests in India: Recent techniques in femicide. Issues in Reproductive and Genetic Engineering. ISSN: 0958-6415.

Patel Vibhuti (2002). Adverse juvenile sex ratio in Kerala. Economic and Political Weekly, June.

Patel Vibhuti (2003). Declining sex ratio and new reproductive technologies. Health Action, July.

Patel Vibhuti (2003). A cultural deficit. India Together, August.

Premi, M.K. & Raju Saraswati (1998). Born to die: Female infanticide in Madhya Pradesh. Search Bulletin, 13 (3).

Premi, M.K. (2001). The missing girl child. Economic and Political Weekly, May 26.

Sen Amartya (1990). More than 100 million women are missing. New York Review of Books, 37 (20).

Sen Amartya (2001). Many faces of gender inequality. Frontline, 18(22), October 27 –November 09.

Sen Amartya (2003). Missing women –Revised. British Medical Journal, 327-1297-1298, December 6.

Siddiqui, F.E & Ranganathan, S. (2001). Handbook on women and human rights – A guide for social activists, Part 1. New Delhi: Kanishka Publishers & Distributors.

Singh Neelam (1998). “Lynching women”- Female foeticide. Health Action, June.

Subrata Lahiri (1974). Preference for sons and ideal family in urban India. Indian Journal of Social Work, 34(4).

Sudha, S. & Rajan, I.S. (1999). Female demographic disadvantage in India 1981-1991: Sex selective abortions and female infanticide: Development and change. Oxford: Blackwell Publishers.

Sulaja, S. (2005). Son preference in the southern states of India: An analysis. Health and Population – Perspectives and Issues, 28 (3), 122-131.

Venkatachalam, R. & Srinivasan, V. (1993). Female infanticide. New Delhi: Har Anand Publications.

REPORTS

Abortion Assessment Project – India.(2003). 'Negative choice', sex determination and sex selective abortion in India. Mallik Rupsa, CEHAT/ Healthwatch.

Census of India (2001). Directorate of Census Operations, Kerala.

First Report on Religion Data (2001). Registrar General and Census Commissioners, India.

Gender and Panchayathiraj: Status of Women in Kerala (2006). Sakhi Women's Resource Centre, Thiruvananthapruam.

GOI (2003). Crime in India. National Crime Records Bureau.

Human Development Report (2001).United Nations Development Programme (UNDP), New York, USA.

ICRW (2000; 2002; 2005). Nation-wide Survey on Domestic Violence in Kerala conducted by Sakhi Resource Centre for Women, Thiruvananthapuram and sponsored by Washington based International Centre for Research on Women.

International Institute for Population Sciences (2000). National Family Health Survey (NFHS II), 1998-99, Mumbai, India, p –122.

Kerala Facts and Figures (2002). State Resource Centre, Thiruvananthapuram, Kerala.

Kerala Study Report (2006). The Kerala Sasthra Sahithya Parishath, September.

Mahila Samakhya Society (2008-09). Status Study of Women in Nilambur Grama Panchayath, Malappuram, Kerala.

Mutharayappa et al. (1997). Son preference and its effect on fertility in India. National Family Health Survey, March 1997.

Patricia Leidl (2005). Silent spring: The tragedy of India's never –born girls. The state of world population 2005. The promise of equality: Gender equity, reproductive health and the Millennium Development Goals, UN Fund for Population Activities.

UNFPA (2005). Gender Based Violence in Kerala, Study commissioned by United Nations Fund for Population Activities through the State Department of Health and conducted by Sakhi Resource Centre for Women, Thiruvananthapuram.

NEWS PAPERS

The Tribune, (2005, September 14). Abortion Act needs to be reviewed says Vyas.

Bums John F (1994, August 27). India fights abortion of female fetuses. New York Times.

Times News Network (2004, April 9). Commitment needed to prevent female foeticide, Chandigarh.

The Hindu (2005, February 19).Decline in child sex ratio among educated sectors.

Kaul Malvika (1993, September 10). Report on death of baby girls. The Pioneer.

International Herald Tribune (2005, November 25). Missing: 50 million Indian girls.

UNPUBLISHED WORKS & PAPER PRESENTATIONS

Glover Jonathan (1994, July). Comments on some ethical issues in sex selection, Unpublished Manuscript presented at the International Symposium on Ethical Aspects of Human Reproduction held in Paris.

Longwe Sara Hlupekile (2002, April). Assessment of the gender orientation of Nepad. Paper presented at the African Forum for Envisioning Africa held in Nairobi, Kenya.

Patel Vibhuthi (2003, April). A cultural deficit. Paper presented at the National Workshop on PNDT Act organized by Centre for Women Development Studies, Delhi at Panaji,Goa.

Sister Gertrude (2005, September). Female foeticide and the trend in Haryana. Seminar report on female foeticide: Challenges and strategies for change. National seminar organized by Sarojini Naidu Centre for Women's Studies, Jamia Millia Islamia, New Delhi.

WEBSITES

www.ernakulam.com
www.genderhealth.org
www.kerala.com
www.malappuram.com
www.merinews.com
www.un..org/rights/dpi1772e.htm

Index